"Reading *Mom Set Free* is like that first breath of fresh air you take after being under water for too long. In this book, Jeannie skillfully shows us how the gospel gives life, freedom, and rest."

—Jessica Thompson, speaker and author of *Everyday Grace*

"There are so many things I love about Jeannie Cunnion. She is funny, she is real, and she isn't afraid to let you know she doesn't have all the answers. As I read *Mom Set Free*, I immediately felt a weight lift off my shoulders. You will find yourself alternately nodding your head and breathing a deep sigh of relief as you turn each page."

—Melanie Shankle, *New York Times* bestselling author and
writer at the blog Big Mama

"Jeannie Cunnion has done something profound with *Mom Set Free* that has the power to not only change your life but the lives of your kids as well. Whether you are a new mom or a seasoned mom, this book will radically impact your parenting. Jeannie won't waste your time with fluff. If you read it slow and open your heart to God's amazing grace, this book will set you radically free."

—Courtney DeFeo, author of *In This House, We Will Giggle* and
creator of the blog Lil Light O' Mine

"As a mom, if you are longing for an exhale this is a must-read! Jeannie includes you in her journey of motherhood, addressing the exhausting paradigms we so easily get stuck in, and then reframing them in the lavish love of God. She beautifully invites you into your own journey—to the heart of the matter—so that you can first receive for yourself what you yearn to pass onto your kids!"

—Lauren Tomlin, wife to worship leader Chris Tomlin

"What we need? *Mom Set Free.* We don't need moms trying harder. We don't need moms doing more. We don't need moms telling each other how it should be done. What our generation is thirsty for—what will change the way we do motherhood and mission—is a whole bunch of moms SET FREE. And what we need right now is a gentle, gracious, humble leader like Jeannie Cunnion to take us there. This book was a balm to my heart and a life-giver to my mothering. I know it will be for you too."

—Jess Connolly, coauthor of *Wild and Free*, author of *Dance Stand Run*,
church planter and teacher, mom of four wild ones

"Jeannie beautifully brings the transforming power of our freedom in Christ into the everyday mission field at our kitchen tables. With sound theology made practical and applicable, *Mom Set Free* takes the pressure off our performance and points us to God's faithfulness through Christ."

—Ruth Chou Simons, mom of six boys, artist, and author of
GraceLaced: Discovering Timeless Truths Through Seasons of the Heart

"*Mom Set Free* should be the book that sits on every mother's nightstand. Read this empowering message, and walk in the freedom you are made for."

—Jennifer Dukes Lee, author of *The Happiness Dare* and *Love Idol*

"Jeannie Cunnion has gently crafted a crucial mothering tool that will empower us moms to preach gospel truth to our own souls, setting us free from the shackles we've allowed to be placed on us. Part heartfelt stories, part scriptural study, this encouraging book will enable you to know and walk in the truth that truly sets you free, so you can parent your children in humility and confidence, resting securely in God's grace."

—Karen Ehman, Proverbs 31 Ministries speaker; *New York Times* bestselling
author of *Keep It Shut* and *Listen, Love, Repeat*; wife; and mom of three

"As a counselor, I sit with weary parents every day—parents who are wearied by the pressure their kids face and wearied by the pressure they face. This weariness trickles out in anxiety, exhaustion, and even anger. And it feels like anything but freedom. But each page of Jeannie's book is entrenched in grace. It will bring not only freedom to each mom who reads it, but it will bring hope—hope that she can be wonderfully, gracefully set free."

—Sissy Goff, M.Ed., LPC, director of child and
adolescent counseling at Daystar Counseling Ministries, Nashville;
speaker; and author of *Are My Kids on Track?*

"If you desire to parent your children with grace, you must first learn to live in grace yourself. This is the message behind Jeannie Cunnion's *Mom Set Free*. Full of the Truth that empowers any mother to overcome the lies of the enemy, *Mom Set Free* releases us to live confidently as we learn to believe that the Lord is not disappointed in us. Jeannie Cunnion doesn't just get it. She shares a practical hope that moves our hearts to freedom. I cannot recommend this book enough."

—Becky Thompson, author
of *Hope Unfolding* and *Love Unending*

"For the mom who frequently hears the voices of guilt and shame around her parenting, for the mom who wonders if God really loves her, for the mom who holds it all together publicly but inside is crumbling: for that mom, it is time to experience freedom. *Mom Set Free* guides us to the kind of freedom that allows us to thrive because we understand how much God loves us. If you want this kind of life-altering freedom, you've come to the right place."

—Alexandra Kuykendall, author *Loving My Actual Life* and cohost of The Open Door Sisterhood podcast

"Ahhh! Parenting can feel so overwhelming, but Jeannie Cunnion's words fill me with the sweet relief of understanding that it's not about what I do but about what God has already done. Cunnion gets it: the worry that you're screwing up your kids, the feeling that you can't breathe. She's been there, and in *Mom Set Free,* she offers insight and wisdom to lead us into fresh air."

—Melanie Dale, author of *It's Not Fair* and *Women Are Scary*

"In *Mom Set Free,* Jeannie uses God's Word to create a beautiful quilt of rest and encouragement while exposing and embracing the heart struggles of every mom. *Mom Set Free* is full of God's unconditional love, affirmation, and Truth for His daughters."

—Wynter Pitts, coauthor of *She Is Yours* and founder of the magazine *For Girls Like You*

"I've been a missionary in Haiti for fifteen years, helping raise the children God has given us, and Jeannie's message of grace and freedom in *Mom Set Free* has changed my life and the way I parent. This book will not only encourage you but point you to Jesus so that you, in turn, can point your children to Him."

—Karris Hudson, field director/vice-president at Danita's Children/Hope for Haiti Children's Center

"While raising my four sons, I have read my fair share of books on how to show God's love and grace to my kids, all the while beating myself up for my imperfections and feeling I have fallen short of being the mom I ought to be. The funny thing is, I don't think I even realized this was happening until I read *Mom Set Free.* Thank you, Jeannie, for sharing God's heart, not just for kids, but indeed for us weary moms. Reading this book has been like a full-body dip in the most refreshing stream of God's love and grace."

—Monica Swanson, writer, Monica Swanson—The Grommom

Mom Set Free

Find Relief from
the Pressure to Get It All Right

JEANNIE CUNNION

Foreword by Elisabeth Hasselbeck

HOWARD BOOKS
AN IMPRINT OF SIMON & SCHUSTER, INC.

NEW YORK   LONDON   TORONTO   SYDNEY   NEW DELHI

Howard Books
An Imprint of Simon & Schuster, Inc.
1230 Avenue of the Americas
New York, NY 10020

First Howard Books trade paperback edition August 2017

HOWARD and colophon are trademarks of Simon & Schuster, Inc.

For information about special discounts for bulk purchases, please contact Simon & Schuster Special Sales at 1-866-506-1949 or business@simonandschuster.com.

The Simon & Schuster Speakers Bureau can bring authors to your live event. For more information or to book an event contact the Simon & Schuster Speakers Bureau at 1-866-248-3049 or visit our website at www.simonspeakers.com.

Design by Jaime Putorti

Manufactured in the United States of America

10 9 8 7

Library of Congress Cataloging-in-Publication Data is available.

ISBN 978-1-5011-5644-1
ISBN 978-1-5011-5645-8 (ebook)

Contents

CONTENTS

CONTENTS

Foreword

We all have a friend who knows exactly how to set up a party; that friend who makes chicken soup when one of our kids is sick, that friend who is honest enough to tell you when you could use a good haircut, the one who listens when there are no words to ease your painful day, the one you can call to pick up your kids from school when you are stuck in line at the grocery store, that friend who cries with you because her heart breaks when yours does, and the friend you can count on to do any of the above—because that is just what friends do.

Jeannie Cunnion has been all that for me and more. She was actually a friend to me before we met. I remember printing out pages from her blog, piling them up by my nightstand and reading them before bed during a time when I desperately needed the wisdom and light that her words offered. Then God brought us together one day in a hallway at church and, in that moment, planted our hearts in fellowship.

As our friendship grew, I witnessed her wrestle with a storm that flooded and stole her home—but *not* her heart. We shared tears inside her minivan after another unthinkable loss, and I watched her immeasurable faith tested and strengthened during a time of great pain. She stayed by my side through some of my toughest days and never failed to help me hold tight to the mast. Soul sisters. That's what we are.

What I love about Jeannie is how real she is—no shimmer over the shatter—simply cracks and brokenness allowing the light of a faithful God to shine through.

She is the girl who—when I am so soaked in worry or shame or hurt or sadness or stress, or when I am being ridiculously hard on myself—redirects my eyes to the truth of Jesus, which sets my heart free again and again. I could not be more excited for you to know the heart, humility, and wisdom of this sweet friend with whom I'm so blessed to do life.

She wrote this book because God first wrote it on her heart.

Meet Jeannie: She doesn't claim or expect perfection. She humbly points to how much we needed the resurrection.

We are different: I eat kale, and she hates anything green. I love being gluten-free, and she sneaks frosting off a cake with lots of glutinous crumbs in it—right in front of me! Secretly I wish I had the guts (literally) to do it.

The beach brings her quiet side out, and college football brings out the loud. Speaking of loud—Mike and her boys make her heart thump.

And through all the countless pizzas, family nights, backyard baseball, and sideline screaming, I have been blessed to call her friend.

She seeks wisdom before speaking. I like that.

She reminds me that I don't need to be any more—that less of me and more of God is always better. I need that.

She is a mom boss—without being bossy.

It moves me to see how brave she is to write about her journey.

She wants you to know that #momming is what we are meant to do.

Throughout these pages, she will remind us all that God smiles when we take flight—kind of like a little mama bird that made its way into my view last year on one of those days when I felt as though the only thing I had mastered was messing everything up!

I'm not one to carry mini-binoculars and go searching for birds. The birdwatchers of this world amaze me with their patience and appreciation for God's little creation. But on that particular day and the days following, I got a glimpse of something God surely wanted me to see.

Each day, a mama bird added to her nest. After some time, I noticed that the nest was actually bigger and that she was making fewer flights out. During this stage, she would sit for what seemed like forever. I knew this meant one thing: eggs!!!

That mama bird and I were now bonded, and I was watching.

One afternoon, some little orange beaks popping up in rotation caught my attention. The mama bird had gone out to do what she needed to do, putting in a hard day's work of finding and bringing worms back to her nest.

There was something pretty neat and simple about this bird. There was something about this bird that I trusted God wanted me to see. I'm fairly sure that God wanted me to observe that this little mama was not worried that the worms she had retrieved weren't good enough or that her feathers weren't as fluffed as the other mom-birds'. She didn't feel guilty that her first-hatched baby bird had not yet spread its wings or that she hadn't had a date night in a while. She didn't feel any pressure about her nest not being clean or peaceful or fancy or big enough, or whether she was even good enough to be a mama bird at all.

Not. At. All. That bird was absolutely confident that she was doing exactly what she was supposed to be doing, and she was sure that her feathers were supposed to be precisely where they were.

That bird was a #MomSetFree. Why couldn't I be more like that? Despite this awesome illustration right before my eyes, I struggled with my "enough-ness," with whether or not I was doing this mom thing just right—and I sometimes still struggle with this.

Thankfully, in this book, Jeannie is going to remind us that freedom in motherhood is what God wants for us. She is gathering a tribe of moms who lean in and hold each other up so we can keep our eyes on this great God who created us to do exactly what we are doing.

Mom Set Free is the assurance that we have a specific mission and that, although this mom thing is not going to be easy, it can be wildly enjoyable.

This is good news, because we have an enemy who wants to steal, kill, and destroy everything God has given us, shackling us into believing the lie that says: *"Because I've had a bad day, I must be a bad mom"*—which is simply not true. Defending against that lie means accepting the invitation to trust that God is holding us, just as we are holding our kids. It means taking up the powerful and blessed mission of raising the children God has entrusted to us while pointing their eyes to the God who loves exactly who they are, exactly where they are.

See, God wants us to raise #KidsSetFree, too!

What I love most of all about this book is that it is not a *have-to, can-do,* or a *should-do.* Rather, *Mom Set Free* is the *created-to-do* anthem of motherhood. So, just like that little mama bird, let's confidently be the moms we were created to be.

He will cover you with his feathers
and under his wings you will find refuge—
his faithfulness will be your armor and protection.
—Psalm 91:4 (NLT)

—Elisabeth Hasselbeck

High Hopes

I had high hopes for the mom I thought I'd be.

For starters, I had a happy childhood, with parents who loved me and led me well. My dad was a pastor, and my mom had a vibrant relationship with God, and together they faithfully taught me—in word and deed—about the love of God in a way that I was eager to emulate in my own parenting. Then, when Mike and I discovered I was pregnant, I quickly bought several parenting books and did my fair share of highlighting and underlining within them. Combining my upbringing and my reading, and a fair dose of determination, I entered parenthood feeling sufficiently equipped to train and discipline and disciple my children, because I've (mostly) been able to accomplish whatever I've set my mind to. Parenting shouldn't be any different, I figured. I mean, how hard can this be?

But then I had children. Three boys in five years, to be exact. Real, moving, breathing, human beings. People who needed me, all of me, all of the time. They needed me to be selfless and kind and patient. They needed me to be all-knowing and awesome. They needed me to be flawless. And they needed all of this while affording me no sleep. Why didn't they care that I needed sleep? I couldn't be awesome when I was exhausted.

It didn't take long for me to discover that the mom I thought I'd be was not the mom I was. This parenting thing was no joke. The formula I applied to the three very unique boys I was desperate to do well by was failing miserably.

While my kids ran circles around me, self-condemning thoughts ran through my mind, convincing me that my weaknesses made me unqualified to raise the children God had entrusted to me, and my failures made me unworthy of God's pleasure in me.

I wouldn't dare share my struggles with any of the moms around me who seemed to have the whole parenting thing mastered. All the while, shame seeped deeper into the crevices of my heart. And the joy with which I always thought I'd parent was mostly displaced by worry and fear.

I couldn't see then what God is helping me see now—how it is actually our *awareness* of our weaknesses that qualifies us for motherhood and keeps us fit for the children God has given us to love and nurture. How our shortcomings remind us to keep our children's eyes fixed on God, not on ourselves. How our struggles are a glorious display of God's greatness, not our own. No, I didn't understand any of that when I first became a mom.

> The pressure to achieve unachievable perfection was on, and I was cracking underneath it.

Instead, the pressure to achieve unachievable perfection was on, and I was cracking underneath it. And I know I'm not the only one.

My fellow mom, we are under so much pressure. We feel the

pressure to be perfect for our kids, the *pressure to perform* for the approval of God, and the *pressure to pretend* we have it all together with other moms. And this pressure leaves us stuck in some pretty awful places and patterns.

But here's the Good News. I believe we can walk in freedom and find relief from the pressure. In fact, I *know* we can! Relief from the pressure that seeks to weigh us down and wipe us out has been freely and generously given to us in the Good News of God's grace. God is inviting us to lay all that pressure down and thrive in what He has actually entrusted to us. He is inviting us to focus on *who He is* rather than *what we aren't*!

He is inviting us to live in freedom *so we can* parent in freedom.

In my previous book, *Parenting the Wholehearted Child*, I wrote about how we can raise children who live in the freedom of being wholeheartedly loved (and liked!) by God in Jesus Christ. It's a very practical book about how to parent with grace.

> I discovered I wasn't the only mom who'd been trying to parent *with* grace without living *in* grace.

But after traveling the country to speak at parenting conferences and women's retreats over the last several years since this book was published, I discovered I wasn't the only mom who'd been trying to parent *with* grace without living *in* grace — without first accepting the grace of God for me, in all of my weakness, sin, and shortcomings. And I discovered I wasn't the only one who struggled to believe God wasn't disappointed in me when I failed to reflect His heart to my children.

It was that discovery that inspired me to write this book.

Friend, to give our kids grace we have to believe and accept

God's grace for us! Because we can't give what we haven't received.

Becoming the mom we want to be doesn't happen by trying harder to be better tomorrow. Becoming the mom we want to be for our children happens as we remember and rest in who Jesus has already been for us! It happens by more deeply believing that the Gospel is for *us*.

Freedom is for *each and every one of us*. God's grace—His unwavering love, unrestrained affection, unconditional acceptance, and unending forgiveness—is given freely and generously in the life, death, and resurrection of Jesus Christ (Romans 3:23–24).

So, *together* we will dive into the bottomless well of God's love for us, we will silence our inner merciless critic, and we will anchor our identities in Christ. We will be set free to live—and parent—in the fullness and abundance of His grace.

Together, we will explore scriptures that reveal how so many of the things we are trying to control are ultimately God's work in our child's life. We will see that we have the privilege of being an instrument of God in that work rather than carrying the responsibility to accomplish that work. We will see that it's ultimately the Holy Spirit's *heart work* not a parent's *hard work* that produces the fruit of the Spirit in our children's lives. And we will see that our job is not to *be* God; it's to point our children *to* God.

> It's ultimately the Holy Spirit's *heart work* not a parent's *hard work* that produces the fruit of the Spirit in our children's lives.

We can stop striving and start thriving in God's grace.

How does God's grace impact our parenting? God's grace frees us *from*:

- shame over our parenting mistakes
- unrealistic expectations of ourselves and our kids
- trying to transform our children's hearts
- manufacturing godly character in our children's lives
- anxiety over whether our children will put their faith in Christ
- feeling like we're not enough
- being defined by our children's success or failure
- using anger or fear to force our children to obey
- fearing that God is disappointed with us when we fail
- worrying that our children will take advantage of grace
- striving to be our children's perfect example and savior

God's grace frees us *to*:

- give our kids the same extravagant grace that Jesus gives us
- be honest about our weaknesses and our need for Christ
- rely on God to melt and mold our children's hearts
- trust the Holy Spirit to produce the fruit of the Spirit in our children's lives

- plant our hope in Christ as the "Author and Perfecter" of our children's faith
- rest in the confidence that Christ *in us* is enough
- anchor our, and our children's, identity in the work of Christ
- weave unconditional love into how we instruct and discipline our kids
- receive the forgiveness of Christ and generously extend it to our kids
- trust that God is sovereign and faithful to His promises
- point our kids to Christ as their perfect example and Savior

All of this is available to each of us, and you, dear mom, are not the exception.

This is an invitation to receive grace, enjoy grace, and soak in grace—because the grace we soak in is the grace that seeps out.

My sincere hope and belief is that this will be a transformative journey that will empower us all to breathe more deeply, walk more lightly, and discover fresh joy in our parenting. Because, on this journey, we will discover that parenting isn't "Do your best, and God will do the rest." God already gave us His best in the person and work of Jesus. We get to rest in *that*!

> The grace we soak in is the grace that seeps out.

"He thought of everything, provided for everything we could possibly need, letting us in on the plans he took such delight in making" (Ephesians 1:7 MSG).

Eugene Peterson writes this about his Christian faith: "It

looks like I'm going to need to let go of what I expected and enter a mystery." I think the same can be said about our parenting. If we want to enjoy the journey, we'll need to let go of those unrealistic expectations we had of ourselves and our kids, and dive into the deep mystery of parenting with open hands and trusting hearts.

So let's not wait another second! And what better place to begin our journey together than in prayer:

> Parenting isn't "Do your best, and God will do the rest." God already gave us His best in the person and work of Jesus.

I pray that from His glorious, unlimited resources He will empower you with inner strength through His Spirit. Then Christ will make His home in your hearts as you trust in Him. Your roots will grow down into God's love and keep you strong. And may you have the power to understand, as all God's people should, how wide, how long, how high, and how deep His love is. May you experience the love of Christ, though it is too great to understand fully. Then you will be made complete with all the fullness of life and power that comes from God. Now all glory to God, who is able, through His mighty power at work within us, to accomplish infinitely more than we might ask or think. Glory to Him in the church and in Christ Jesus through all generations forever and ever! Amen.
—Ephesians 3:16–21 NLT

PART ONE

The Pressure's On!

CHAPTER 1

The Pressure to Be Enough

The Freedom to Rely on the "Enough-ness" of Christ

During my first pregnancy, I can clearly remember people—friends and strangers alike—telling me how much I would love being a mom. How I would love my son *so much* that I would feel like my heart would burst. And they were right. The moment the nurse laid my newborn son's bare body on my chest and I felt his heart beat against mine, I knew there was nothing in this world I wouldn't do for him. My instantaneous love for him overwhelmed me.

That newborn baby is now a teenager, and I am *still* caught off guard by how the very sight of him, along with his three younger brothers, slays me.

However, what I *don't* remember anyone telling me before my first son was born is that motherhood would not only enlarge my heart but it would also expose all my weaknesses and inadequacies, and that there would be days when I'd feel so desperate that I wouldn't even recognize myself. I didn't see *that* coming. I didn't expect that motherhood would reveal both the beautiful *and* the not-so-beautiful parts of my heart.

What I Wish I'd Known

I recently attended a baby shower for a young woman named Nicole. She was a soon-to-be first-time mom and a woman I very much admire and adore. To call her wise beyond her years would be an understatement.

The shower was a joyous occasion, as all baby showers are, but the joy at this shower was palpable. Nicole and her husband, Jimmy, had long prayed and hoped for this "miracle baby" whom we were all eager to embrace and celebrate.

> I didn't expect that motherhood would reveal both the beautiful *and* the not-so-beautiful parts of my heart.

However, just about halfway through the celebration, I felt a strong inclination to pull my friend aside and warn her that parenting isn't all petits fours, pink lemonade, and filtered Instagram photos. Perhaps it was because I was on the tail end of a very defeating week of parenting. The kind where my joy was lost in the battles. Failures outweighed victories. Fighting trumped kindness. All my intentionality felt worthless. And I was mentally and physically wiped out.

You'll be happy to know I didn't ruin the shower. I focused on the gift this child will be to Nicole and Jimmy. But soon thereafter, Nicole and I grabbed coffee and, because I love her, I shared with her some of the things I wish I'd known as a new mom.

I said things like:

This parenting thing is hard. Really hard. And there will be a lot of mornings when you want to pull the covers over your head and stay in bed because you don't have the mental, physical, or emotional strength to meet the demands of the day and be the mom you want to be.

And when you do muster up the strength to put your feet on the floor and take that one next step, you will want to say, with the little energy you can summon, "Who wants to play hide and seek? Doesn't that sound like fun! Okay, so you go hide, and be sure to find a really great spot where I've never found you before, and Mommy will come look for you after I count to five hundred." Yes, you will do this because you are falling apart. It won't mean you don't love your children with all you have. It just means you're human. And that's okay.

And you will make mistakes. Lots of them. And you will have regrets. Big ones. And you will need Jesus like you've never needed Him before!

But, girlfriend, what I most want to tell you is this: On the days when you feel like you're *not enough*, hold on tight to the truth that you have a Savior who *is enough*. And what is hard for you is not hard for Him! So run to Him. Rely on Him. Depend on Him.

Isn't *that* what we most want to hear?

We all need another mom to affirm the "crazy" we feel. We

need to know that we're not the only one whose fierce love for our children coexists with feelings of failure and desperation.

What is hard for us is not hard for God.

We all need another mom to remind us—over and over again—that we have a powerful God who has given us His perfect son, Jesus Christ. And He is our enough.

The Relief God Promises

When we're feeling pushed far beyond our human limitations, and we look in the mirror only to find our face worn and weary with the day's demands, we can turn to God's Word and read the relief God promises.

O Jacob, how can you say the Lord does not see your troubles?
O Israel, how can you say God ignores your rights?
Have you never heard?
Have you never understood?
The Lord is the everlasting God,
the Creator of all the earth.
He never grows weak or weary.
No one can measure the depths of his understanding.
He gives power to the weak and strength to the powerless.
Even youths will become weak and tired, and
young men will fall in exhaustion.
But those who trust in the Lord will find new strength.
They will soar high on wings like eagles.

They will run and not grow weary.
They will walk and not faint.
(40: 27–31 NLT)

Did you get all that? There's a lot of *relief* packed into this passage:

- God does not lose track of us.
- God very much cares what happens to us.
- God's knowledge and understanding cannot be measured.
- God never grows weak or weary.
- He knows everything. Every. Single. Thing.
- He gives power to the weak.
- He gives strength to the powerless.

What we learn through the words of Isaiah is that *who God is*, which is sovereign, and *what He gives* us, which is grace, is enough. And He wants us to trust Him. When we're exhausted—both mentally *and* physically—He wants us to rely on Him to be all that we need. He wants us to recognize that parenting is actually meant to—*designed to*—deepen our dependence on Him. He is wooing our hearts closer and closer to His in and through our kids.

> Parenting is designed to deepen our dependence on God.

God actually has a simple but profound message for us regarding our quest to be *enough*. In Psalms 46:10, His voice breaks through and proclaims, "Be still and know that I am God."

I have clung to this verse for years. In fact, I most love the New American Standard translation that says, "Cease striving and know that I am God." I've recently discovered something that makes this verse even more meaningful to me. The Hebrew meaning for "be still" is *"enough."* Oh, how profound this is for our lives and for our parenting. He is saying, *Enough of trying to be enough!*

The Squeeze of Vertical and Horizontal Pressure

Whether you're in the middle of raising tiny babies, tantruming toddlers, tenacious teenagers, or adult kids, you're likely well acquainted with the hopeless feeling of being "not enough" for your children. But here's the thing. As we seek to overcome the pressure we feel to be enough for our kids, we also have to take an honest look at the pressure we feel to be enough for God. See, most of us aren't just trying to be enough for our kids, which is the horizontal pressure we feel. We're also trying to be enough for God, and that's the vertical pressure I want us to talk about honestly on this journey together.

Do you ever fear (or maybe the better question is, how *often* do you fear?) that you are disappointing God with your personal failures and your parenting mistakes? That pressure usually leads us to do one of two things. With clenched fists and gritted teeth, we *try harder* to keep God happy and not lose His love and acceptance. Or, we *give up* because we assume God has given up on us. Neither of which draws us closer to His heart, where He wants us to hear Him saying, "I don't need you to impress me. I want you to rely on me."

And when it comes to parenting—where we experience the horizontal pressure to prove we're enough—we just keep searching for newer and better ways to control our child's behavior, secure our child's success, or change our child's heart. And none of it works—at least, not for long.

Is it any wonder that under all this pressure we *crack*?

Are you tired of being the mom who is barely stumbling along, crushed under the pressure to be "enough"? Are you tired of feeling that you can't catch your breath, can't keep up, and can't be all that your children need you to be? *Are you tired of being tired?*

I get it.

The Enough-ness of Christ

I spent entirely too long trying to prove to myself, to God, and to everybody around me that I was enough. Only in recent years have I begun to understand what Paul meant when he said that in our pursuit to be enough, we deny and reject the work of Christ—it's as if "Christ died for nothing" (Galatians 2:21 NIV). In other words, if we ever had *a shot* at being enough, then everything Jesus endured on our behalf to reconcile us to God was pointless. God never called us to be enough. Not for Him and not for our kids. Not for our spouse and not for our church. He calls us to be loved. To be His beloved. This title has been gifted to us and can never be taken away from us. All because of Jesus. So we can stop trying to be enough because Jesus was, and is, our more than enough.

> God never called us to be enough. He calls us to be His beloved.

So the next time we wrestle with the question "Am I enough?" rather than try to justify our enough-ness, let's see our question as a cue to re-call the preeminence of Christ in our lives and our daily mothering. We can unashamedly proclaim, as Charles Spurgeon once said, *"I have a great need for Christ. I have a great Christ for my need."* It is only in this confession—"I have a great need for Christ"—that we are relieved from the guilt of not being all we desire to be for our kids. It is then that we become grateful for all that Christ already is for them.

Jesus freed us from trying to prove that we are enough. He lived a sinless life, died a sinless death, conquered the grave, and has freely given us His perfect record (Romans 3:23–25 NIV). When we are in Christ, there is nothing to prove. Let *that* sink into your weary and worn-out soul.

We get to rest in the assurance of God's grace and His sovereignty over us and over the kids we long to love and lead well. We are free!

An Invitation

Rest assured, when I say "We are free" I don't mean we've been given an excuse to be a lazy or lousy parent. This is not a permission slip to give up. This is not an *out*. This is an *in*.

An invitation to:

- lay down what God has not asked us to carry so we thrive in what He has
- embrace our significance *in light of* God's sovereignty
- discover God's acceptance of us and affection for us, just as we are
- receive God's grace so we can reflect God's heart to our kids
- stop trying so hard and start enjoying our kids more
- weave grace into how we discipline our kids
- trust God with the kids He has entrusted to us
- become more of the moms we long to be for our kids

An invitation to trust that "everything that goes into a life of pleasing God has been miraculously given to us by getting to know, personally and intimately, the One who invited us to God. The best invitation we ever received!" (2 Peter 1:3–4 MSG).

We have been personally invited—by name—to walk in freedom from the pressure to be "enough"—for our children *and* for God.

Let's turn now to see how this freedom applies to some of the immense pressure we face in our daily mothering!

CHAPTER 2

The Pressure to Be the Perfect Example

The Freedom to Point Our Children to the Example of Christ

Be the person you want your children to become."

If you're a mom, it's unlikely you've escaped that well-intentioned advice. No pressure there, right?

Be perfectly patient, perfectly calm, perfectly thankful, perfectly loving, perfectly joyful, perfectly kind . . . so that your children will overflow with the same . . . *perfection*. Yes. That.

In other words, "perfect parenting in = perfect kids out."

That's the equation that drove me to despair and nearly stole all the joy in my parenting, because I was confident I wasn't modeling perfection. I wasn't even close.

No matter where we are on the parenting spectrum, we feel the pressure to get it all right so our kids will turn out all right. But, at the very same time, we are painfully aware of our weaknesses, our shortcomings, our brokenness, and the ways in which we get it wrong. That leaves us in perpetual fear that our kids will turn out wrong—or worse, have *already* turned out wrong. And it's too late to get it right now.

Fear of Disappointing God and Harming Our Kids

On how many days have you been ashamed of who you've become and how you've treated your kids? On how many days have you felt desperate and terrified that you're disappointing God because you're struggling to parent the kids you love like you always imagined you would? If you're anything like me, the answer is "too many."

Like when my son overheard me say an unkind thing about a woman who had been gossiping about me, and I realized I wasn't modeling how to love our enemies and bless those who persecute us.

> We feel the pressure to get it all right so our kids turn out all right.

Like when I yelled at my boys to stop yelling at each other, and I realized I was modeling the very thing I was instructing them to stop doing.

Like when I lost my patience with my son for not listening to me, and I realized I was crushing his spirit rather than gently but firmly correcting his disobedience.

And that was all in one day.

Friend, the struggle is real. Every single day I am confronted with my humanity and fallen nature.

I never expected to get so much wrong, and I never expected to feel so little hope.

And yet, I'm beginning to understand why I do.

God Is Relying on Me?

See, our enemy Satan works tirelessly to make us believe that God is relying on us to be the perfect example for our kids to follow. Why? So we will keep our hope anchored in ourselves rather than in Christ. He knows that our mere trying harder to be better tomorrow will steal our joy, kill our hope, and destroy the freedom Jesus calls us to walk in. Any time our eyes are turned inward for hope rather than upward, we will despair (Hebrews 12:2 NIV).

Here's the thing about parenting that took me entirely too long to figure out (I can be a *very* slow learner): God doesn't only work through us to grow our children. He works through *them* to grow *us*.

He works through them to make us *run to* and *rely on* Him to be who we can never be for our children, and to accomplish what we can never accomplish in our children.

See, parenting is not about God relying on us to be perfect examples for our kids to follow. Parenting is about us relying on God to captivate our child's heart despite all our mistakes. And so much of the pressure we experience stems from us getting this backward!

For example, Proverbs 22:6 says,

> Parenting is not about God relying on us to be perfect examples for our kids to follow. Parenting is about us relying on God to captivate our child's heart despite all our mistakes.

"Bring up a child by teaching him the way he should go, and when he is old he will not turn away from it" (NLV). Now, what I've come to discover is that most of us read this verse as an *if-then* promise—*if* we train up our children correctly, *then* they will not turn away from our teaching.

This puts us under immense pressure, thinking our child's future is riding solely on our performance. Our mentality is either, "It's all about me, and if I get it mostly right, my kids will stay on the right path," *or* "It's all about me, and if I get it mostly wrong, my kids will turn down the wrong path." But we need to remember that this proverb is just that—it's a *proverb*, not a *promise*.

Hear this insight from the *ESV Gospel Transformation Bible* on this proverb:

> The proverbs provide reliable guidance, but they do not address every contingency encountered in a sinful world. Even the best parenting can result in a prodigal son and a prideful son (Luke 15:11–32). Ultimately the way a child "should go" is not a college or career choice but an eternal choice to live for God. Such a way is profoundly influenced by parents' actions but is ultimately determined by the child's heart.[1]

Yes, What We Do and Say Matters

Now, this isn't to suggest that we parents don't play a crucial role in the healthy development of our kids. Of course, we do. What we do and what we say absolutely matters. Our actions can hurt or heal. Our words can build up or tear down. What we model has an enormous impact on the thought patterns and behavior of our children. And we are wise to remember that how they see us living our lives is even more influential than what they hear us saying with our mouths.

Therefore, we should seek to model what it looks like to live in the likeness of Christ to the very best of our ability and to heed the instruction Paul gave Titus when he wrote, "And you yourself must be an example to them by doing good works of every kind. Let everything you do reflect the integrity and seriousness of your teaching" (Titus 2:7 NLT).

Here Paul is emphasizing to Titus that the example he sets should foster rather than frustrate the spread of the gospel in the lives of people in Crete. Similarly, our lifestyle should foster rather than frustrate our children's understanding of what it means to follow Christ.

But! This is what we must remember: Our children don't need us to be the *perfection* of Christ. They need to see us in *pursuit* of Christ. They need us to *point* them to Christ.

See, I'm actually okay with "being the person I want my children to become" *if* that person is someone who is:

> Our children don't need us to be the *perfection* of Christ. They need to see us in *pursuit* of Christ.

- desperately aware of her sin and shortcomings
- deeply grateful for her Savior
- daily desiring (but not always succeeding) to walk in obedience to Christ through the power of the Holy Spirit

Our children need to know that there is only One who has never and will never let them down. And that One isn't us. It's Jesus. Because as hard as we try to be good examples for our children to follow, we will fail. But confessing this does not make us failures. It makes us free! Free from the pressure to be who Jesus has already been for them. It makes us free from the hopelessness in which we get stuck. It makes us people who are truly grateful for God's redeeming grace that is bigger than our biggest mistakes.

> I can trust God with the kids He has entrusted to me as I seek to raise them to His glory, not mine.

When we understand this great truth, we can think, "It's not all about me. I am significant, but I am not God. I can trust God with the kids He has entrusted to me as I seek to raise them to His glory, not mine."

An Invitation from Jesus

If you've been wearing yourself out trying to be the person you want your children to become by relying mostly on yourself and very little on God, I want you to lean in and read the following invitation. My fellow mom, this is an invitation *from Jesus*. These are His words, not mine.

But please do me a favor. Before you begin reading, insert your name at the beginning of the verse.

_____, are you tired? Worn out? Burned out on religion? Come to me. Get away with me and you'll recover your life. I'll show you how to take a *real rest*. Walk with me and work with me—watch how I do it. Learn the *unforced rhythms of grace.* I won't lay anything heavy or ill-fitting on you. Keep company with me and you'll learn to live *freely and lightly*. (Matthew 11:28–30 MSG, emphasis added)

Freely and lightly. Doesn't just the very idea of living "freely and lightly" make you take a long deep breath of relief?

Or maybe it makes you skeptical. Maybe you think, "I am under way too much pressure and falling way too short to ever live freely and lightly as a mom in this season of my parenting. There is entirely too much I need to do. There are meals to cook. Bottoms to wipe. College applications to complete. Schedules to coordinate. Carpools to run. Hugs to give. Appointments to make. Games to watch. iPhones to check. And that's just the easy stuff. Don't even get me started on the hard and complicated stuff."

If that's you, oh, I get it. I really do. But, Jesus *never* invites us into anything He does not make good on. He is a promise keeper through and through. And He is inviting us to live freely and lightly, *amidst* the pressure.

Jesus is inviting us to live as moms set free! Yes, you and me—the moms who are burned out from trying to get it all right and exhausted from the heavy burdens and worries we carry.

He wants to show us how to take a "real rest" as we "keep company with Him" and learn His "unforced rhythms of grace."

The *real rest* that Jesus is talking about here isn't simply a good long nap while the kids are at school or off at Grandma's for the weekend. Although that would be fantastic! It's not a rest in which you simply clear the kid's calendar and cancel all your plans. Although sometimes, that would also be fantastic!

The kind of rest Jesus offers is much more profound. It's much more permanent than the post-nap refreshment that fades as fast as the caffeine rush from our morning coffee(s). This rest is one where our soul is at rest *in the midst of motherhood.* Our children *need* us to seek this rest!

In fact, recent research confirms that rest matters when it comes to parenting. A *Washington Post* article reported that

> [when] mothers in particular are stressed, sleep-deprived, guilty and anxious . . . that mothers' distress is related to poor outcomes for their children," including behavioral and emotional problems. Indeed, some of that stress, the researchers say, may be driven by what they call "intensive mothering"— beliefs that have ratcheted up the standards for what it takes to be considered a good mother in recent decades.[2]

I don't share this research with you to make you *distressed about being distressed,* but to encourage you to *lean on Jesus* in a real way. When you keep company with Christ, you will—you can't not be—strengthened and changed from the inside out (Romans 12:2).

You have been set free from being perfect for your children. Jesus has already accomplished a perfection that you can rest in. To parent in the "unforced rhythms of His grace," we need to accept the Good News that our children's hearts are not wholly dependent on our performance as a parent. We need to accept that what we get right and what we get wrong is not what will ultimately determine who our children will become!

> Our children's hearts are not wholly dependent on our performance as a parent.

As if all this weren't enough, God has given us His Spirit to help us be more of who we want to be.

Don't Try This Alone

Not long ago, after having to ask my boys repeatedly to complete their tasks so we could get out the door on time, I shouted, "Boys, I am running out of patience with you!" But before I could speak another word, the thought ran through my mind: *Aren't you glad God never runs out of patience with* you? And I enjoyed sharing it with my kids. I was able to use that small moment in the middle of our chaotic day to remind my kids of the Good News that "God never runs out of patience for us. He never comes to the end of His rope with us."

Sometimes we're tempted to think that because we continue to sin, God gets a little more disappointed in us and a little more annoyed with us until He finally just throws His hands up and declares, "I'm giving up on you altogether." But that's not God. Out of His fullness, He gives us grace upon grace (John 1:16).

Let's remember who Christ is for us, and then let's rely on the Holy Spirit to be our guide.

> *So I say, let the Holy Spirit guide your lives. Then you*
> *won't be doing what your sinful nature craves. The sinful*
> *nature wants to do evil, which is just the opposite of what*
> *the Spirit wants. And the Spirit gives us desires that are*
> *the opposite of what the sinful nature desires. These two*
> *forces are constantly fighting each other, so you are not*

free to carry out your good intentions . . . But the Holy
Spirit produces this kind of fruit in our lives: love, joy,
peace, patience, kindness, goodness, faithfulness, gentleness,
and self-control. There is no law against these things!
(Galatians 5:16–17, 22–23 NLT)

You know the expression "Don't try this at home"? In our parenting, it's "Don't try this *alone*." We *cannot* be the examples we long to be without the indwelling power of the Holy Spirit. And, as we'll see in the next chapter, we don't have to!

CHAPTER 3

The Pressure to Be in Control

The Freedom of Believing That God Is Sovereign

I'm part of a text string with several moms who are also in the trenches with kids of various ages. We mostly use this string as an opportunity to share our personal insecurities and parental agony, knowing that those who reply will pray, cheer, and share similar stories of struggle. This isn't "misery loves company" as much as it is "moms love company"—emotional company. Someone to say, "I get it. God's got us. I'm here for you, friend."

We feel overwhelmed by the magnitude of influence we carry, and we feel terribly inadequate to help our children navigate the hardships they face. We know we've got only one shot at this, and we desperately want to get it right for them.

But while we're doing the very best we can to raise overcomers and world changers and to help our kids navigate this life with confidence and humility, we mostly just feel like we're drowning. There is so much we can't prevent or fix. It hurts to see our kids hurt.

We hurt when our kids battle eating disorders, substance abuse, or severe depression. Or when they get diagnosed with a life-threatening illness or face brutal bullying or peer rejection. We hurt when their hearts get broken, or they don't make the team. Our hearts ache when they insist on making decisions that lead to destruction, or when they simply look in the mirror and feel unworthy of love and belonging.

We desperately want to know what to do and what to say to make it all okay. But there isn't always an easy fix, and life isn't always okay. Motherhood can rip your heart out, can't it?

That's why we can't go any further in this discussion without spending some time with Romans 8:28.

We desperately want to know what to do and what to say to make it all okay. But there isn't always an easy fix, and life isn't always okay.

All Things Work Together for Good

Here, the apostle Paul makes the simple—but complex—affirmation:

God causes everything to work together for the good of those who love God and are called according to his purpose for them (Romans 8:28, NLT).

This verse can relieve a lot of pressure, but it also unearths a lot of questions, which is why entire books have been written and entire sermon series have been preached on it. So in these next few pages, I want to walk humbly alongside you as we explore some "guiding principles" that help us understand what it means for *our kids* that "God causes everything to work together for the good of those who love God."

Guiding Principle #1: We All Have Free Will

Let's start with this basic truth: God has given our children free will, and they are responsible for their choices. It's essential that our children understand this. Their choices matter. Likewise, *we* have free will and *our* choices matter. But! God is not limited by our choices. That's good news! And He makes everything work out according to plan and in conformity with the purpose of his perfect will (Ephesians 1:11).

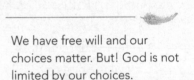

We have free will and our choices matter. But! God is not limited by our choices.

Guiding Principle #2: Not Everything "Happens for a Reason"

The truth that God works all *together for good* does not mean that "everything happens for a reason." This is not what the apostle Paul is saying in Romans 8:28. He is not saying that the most tragic of events are "meant to be," and he is not trying to put a silver lining on a tragic story.

Guiding Principle #3: God Is Not the Author of Evil

For all that we *do not* know, we *do* know that God is not the author of evil. Scripture tells us that "every good and perfect gift is from above, coming down from the Father of the heavenly lights, who does not change like shifting shadows" (James 1:17 NIV). Think back to the beauty and peace and health of the Garden of Eden. This was God's original intent for humankind. God is not the author of evil. Rather, "He is the Rock, his works are perfect, and all his ways are just. A faithful God who does no wrong, upright and just is he (Deuteronomy 32:4 NIV).

This means God does not cause our suffering for a "higher purpose." Rather, all of the sin that bubbles up from inside us and all of the sin that is committed against us can be used for good by God. He can repurpose for good that which the enemy intended for evil (Genesis 50:20).

Guiding Principle #4: God Is Present in Our Pain

What is even more astounding is that God is present in our pain. "If your heart is broken, you'll find God right there; if you're kicked in the gut, he'll help you catch your breath" (Psalm 34:18 MSG).

He does not abandon us in our pain. He actually enters into our pain. Not because He has to, but because He wants to. He loves us that much.

God intimately knows our suffering and can be trusted to carry us through it.

So like the psalmist we can, with assurance, pray, "Lord, 'You keep track of all my sorrows. You have collected all my tears in your bottle. You have recorded each one in your book' " (Psalm 56:8 NLT).

Our suffering is not lost on God. And our suffering does not signify the loss of His love.

When circumstances seem cruel and all hope feels lost, we must remember that our God—who doesn't always make sense to our finite human understanding—is, Himself, well acquainted with parental agony. He knows the torment of watching His child suffer, and yet, as Romans 8:32 goes on to remind us, He "did not keep His own Son for Himself but gave Him for us all. Then with His Son, will He not give us all things?" (Romans 8:32 NLT).

> God intimately knows our suffering and can be trusted to carry us through it.

Everything is filtered through the love—*the love*—of the Father.

What GOOD Is God Working Toward?

So what *is* the good toward which God is working? We find the answer in the following verse: His purpose is that we "be conformed to the image of His son" (Romans 8:29 NIV). He is working all things together to draw our hearts closer to His and transform us more into the likeness of Christ.

See, of all the things we want to give our kids and be for our kids, let us not miss the one thing that matters above everything else—pointing them to God.

When I feel angst about the daily (sometimes big, sometimes

small) struggles our boys have, it helps me to remember the simple but profound wisdom of Ann Voskamp: "Think of eternity—and live backward from that."[1] That puts things in perspective for me every time, and so much of what stresses me out begins to slip away in light of eternity.

I know it doesn't always feel like God is working things together for good. In the dark night of the soul, in the utter heartbreak, in the pit of despair, being told that God works everything together for good feels like a fluffy, worthless, and sometimes even infuriating promise. Trust me, I know. There is so very much that we will never fully understand on this side of heaven.

But this I also know: *God's infinite grace and wisdom is far beyond our human comprehension.* And for that I am exceptionally grateful. Who wants to worship a God whose greatness you can grasp? For the Lord God says, "I am the First and the Last, the beginning and the end of all things. I am the All-powerful One Who was and Who is and Who is to come" (Revelation 1:8 NLV).

But as we expectantly wait for that day when God will make everything as it should be, we can have full confidence that He is in control and that He knows *exactly* what He is doing. Indeed, "Every day was written before one of them came to be. . . . Every moment was laid out before a single day had passed" (Psalm 139:16 NLT).

We can have full confidence that He goes *with* our children and that He is *for* our children, and that somehow, some way, He is working all things together for good. We may not see it now. But we must seek to have faith, or we will be paralyzed by the pressure.

We Are Instruments of God's Grace

What I find so beautiful, so humbling, and perhaps, at times, so frightening, is that God chooses to use *us*—to involve *us*—as His instruments in the lives of our children. But! He is not asking us to play His role. Why is this so important to remember? Because *when we forget God's sovereignty, we will more likely parent with:*

- worry
- fear
- control
- anger
- pride
- shame

Our posture will be clenched fists, trying to hold it all together.

When we remember God's sovereignty, we will more likely parent with:

- wonder
- faith
- connection
- gentleness and self-control
- humility
- unconditional love

Our posture will be open-handed, ready to receive and give grace.

Here's how our lists look side by side:

- worry or wonder
- fear or faith
- control or connection
- anger or gentleness and self-control
- pride or humility
- shame or unconditional love

We have only to glance at these lists to know where we want to be. Our backs are breaking and our shoulders are tight. We long for a lighter load. And, Momma, let me assure you, we *can* have what we long for.

Rather than be ruled by worry, we can live in wonder—hopeful curiosity and expectation—of what God is doing in the lives of our kids. Rather than be ruled by fear, we can live by faith, "being sure we will get what we hope for and being sure of what we cannot yet see" (Hebrews 11:1 NLV). Rather than parenting by trying to control our children, we can parent by seeking connection with them. Rather than allow anger, pride, and shame to overflow into our parenting, we can lead our children in gentleness, humility, and love. Further into our journey we will dig deeper into how we move from one to the other. But for now, let it be said that the shift starts with accepting this burden-lifting, game-changing truth: *God did not choose you to be your children's Savior. He chose you to be their parent.* And He will equip you to parent the children He's gifted to you.

> God did not choose you to be your children's Savior. He chose you to be their parent.

We don't do our children, or ourselves, any favors by believing otherwise.

Our enemy wants to crush us under the pressure of trying to be our child's Savior. It thrills him to no end to see us trying to play God in our child's life because he knows the fruit it will produce. But God doesn't need us to "play God." Rather, God has commissioned us to be *instruments of grace* in the work He is doing in the lives of our kids *while we rest in the assurance* that He already has covered what we are trying so hard to control!

In fact, Proverbs 16:9 is quite clear on this. "We can make our plans, but the Lord determines our steps" (NLT).

Of course, we *can* and *must* help our kids face the battles they have to fight and the mountains they have to climb. We *can* and *must* do hard things for our kids. Our hearts *should* beat fierce and strong as we fight on the front lines for our kids.

> Our insufficiency bears witness to the total sufficiency of Christ.

But in the fight, we must remember where our strength and courage come from when we do the hard things. And it's not from our superhero capes. It comes from God. We can face anything, alongside our kids, knowing that it is *in* Christ that we are strengthened. Our insufficiency bears witness to the total sufficiency of Christ (2 Corinthians 3:5). Our human weakness reveals God's divine strength. We are the weary. Jesus—who conquered the grave—is our great Overcomer.

Will You Trust Me?

One of our sons endured a deeply painful season of feeling rejection and "un-belonging." It was a culmination of events that came to a head on one particular evening when my husband and I bore witness to it. And it broke my heart in ways I didn't know it could be broken. After our boys went to bed that evening, we curled up together under our sheets, and I sobbed into my husband's strong arms, "My heart is broken. I wish I could switch places with him and absorb his pain. I know I can't rescue him from real life and that he needs to learn how to navigate these situations in order to grow in character and resiliency. I know God will use this in his life in ways I can't see now. I know. But I hate it. It's killing me."

Also feeling the heaviness of our son's sadness, Mike pulled me close and assured me, "I know. But we just need to keep on praying, Wifey. We keep on speaking God's truth into his life, we keep on guiding him to the best of our ability, and we keep on trusting that God's got this. He's an extraordinary boy, and God's not done with him yet. Not even close."

See, while my husband's words weren't earth shattering, they were exactly what I needed to hear in that moment. Those are the words, I believe, that God wants you and me to hear in so much of our daily parenting. God wants us to lean in and listen close as He says, "I've got this. Just like I've always had this. And by the way, I can do immeasurably more than you could ever ask for or imagine (Ephesians 3:20). Will you trust me?"

I have a long way to go in learning to let go and trust God with my children, but this I can assure you: My desperate need to feel like I'm wise enough or strong enough or good enough to lead my kids through the hardships they will inevitably encounter and the big decisions they will have to make is decreasing as I remember what the Lord said through Isaiah in 55:8 (ESV):

> *My thoughts are not your thoughts, neither are your ways*
> *my ways, declares the Lord. For as the heavens are higher*
> *than the earth, so are my ways higher than your*
> *ways, and my thoughts than your thoughts.*

When we find ourselves crumbling under the pressure to hold all things together, that's a good indicator that we have forgotten the supremacy of Christ, who is "the image of the invisible God, the firstborn of all creation. For by him all things were created . . . and in him all things hold together" (Colossians 1:15–17 NIV). Friend, can I remind you of something I need to be reminded of on a daily basis? God is the One holding it all together. Not us.

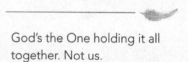

God's the One holding it all together. Not us.

It's ironic, really, that it's easier to try to play God than it is to surrender to God.

But just imagine how much deeper we'd breathe (and how much better we'd sleep!) if we loosened our grip, trusted God to be enough for our kids, and walked in faith in His good plans for them! Just imagine.

CHAPTER 4

The Pressure to Transform Our Children's Hearts

The Freedom of Trusting God with the Children He's Entrusted to Us

Mommy, does Jesus live in your heart?" That's the question a precious seven-year-old girl asked her mom after they'd finished their nighttime prayers.

The mom stroked her daughter's hair, looked tenderly into her daughter's eyes, and assured her, "He sure does, sweetie. Jesus has been in my heart since I was a young child like you."

"Mommy," her daughter continued with childlike curiosity, "what does Jesus do in there?"

Don't you just love how literal our kids can be? This sweet little girl is trying to envision Jesus just chillin' out inside her mom's heart.

Her mom replied, "The same thing He's doing in your heart, honey. He's making me more like Him."

The Heart: The Source of Our Being

When we think about the heart, we tend to think of it as merely the place from which our emotions flow. But Scripture paints a much bigger picture. God's Word describes the heart as the place from which emotions, thoughts, motivation, plans, decisions, and ultimately action flow. No wonder Proverbs 4:23 provides this wise instruction regarding the heart: "Above all else, guard your heart, for *everything* you do flows from it" (NIV). Not some things. Everything.

Luke 6:45 also addresses this idea of heart overflow. Here Jesus says, "What you say flows from what is in your heart" (NLT). This is one reason so much emphasis is put on focusing on our child's heart in our parenting—because the heart is the center of our child's spirit. But here's the important thing we have to remember when we focus on parenting our child's heart. There is only One who can transform it. And that one isn't you and it isn't me. It's Jesus. We can shepherd a child's heart, but we are powerless to transform it.

I must admit, at first I saw this as very bad news. I didn't like feeling powerless. I wanted to get inside my kids' hearts and do some prioritizing and producing. I wanted to believe that if I put all the right stuff in, all the right stuff would come out. But it was only a matter of time before I realized that I can't manufacture virtues in their lives any more than I can do that in my own. Rather, loving and living like Christ will be the manifestation of God's grace in their hearts. Like the mother said to her daughter, it is Jesus—by grace, through the power of the Holy Spirit—who makes us more like Him.

Now here's what embracing this truth does. It inclines us to take a good, long look at the significance of our role in our children's lives *in light of* God's sovereignty over their lives. And, hopefully, it ultimately inclines us to *surrender* the hearts of our kids into the hands of our all-powerful and all-loving God. When we remember God's sovereignty, we stop wanting to write our child's story, and we become thankful God never gave us the pen.

> When we remember God's sovereignty, we stop wanting to write our child's story, and we become thankful God never gave us the pen.

In truth, we are powerless over the hearts of our kids. We can spend a lifetime fighting this reality, or we can wise up and embrace it. But how we do that is the tricky part. How do we get comfortable with laying things down that we have gotten so used to carrying? How do we get okay with trusting God with what we have tried so hard to control?

So this is the fun part. We are going to dive deeply into a few passages to see what God's Word has to say about this—about *His role and our role*, about *our incompetence and His competence*, about *our significance in light of His sovereignty*. It's only when we believe how very much "God's got it" that we can be free from the pressure.

What are some of the things we attempt to carry and control as Christian parents? We'll need to get really honest here. Will you pause for a moment and think about your answer?

Okay, ready for my list? Oh wait, before I do that, I want to say this: Please read this list knowing full well that in the next two chapters we will talk about what we actually have been called by God to do as parents. I am not negating the very important role we play in each of the things I am about to list. But here, I want to encourage us to *start* by recognizing our role, our significance, *in light of* God's role and sovereignty.

My Child's Salvation

The first thing on my "pressure" list was my kids' *salvation*. I felt the pressure to lead my children to a saving faith—to *ensure* that they put their trust in Jesus at a young age. Not gonna lie—I want eternity with them. More than anything else, I want eternity with them. But I also want them to experience the abundant life Jesus Christ came to give them in the here and now.

But I am set free from the pressure when I turn to God's Word and remember what Jesus said:

For no one can come to me unless the Father who sent me draws them to me, and at the last day I will raise them up.
(John 6:44 NLT)

This means that my kids will not come to Christ solely on their own initiative, and they will certainly not come to Christ solely on mine. It will be only through the Father giving them the desire to come to Christ. The Father must draw my children to His heart. I can't push and plead them there. Rather, He pursues them and woos them to Himself.

Two other verses that bring great relief from the pressure to produce a saving faith:

The Lord is not slow about keeping His promise as some people think. He is waiting for you. The Lord does not

want any person to be punished forever. He wants all
people to be sorry for their sins and turn from them.
(2 Peter 3:9 NLV)

Even before he made the world, God loved us and chose
us in Christ to be holy and without fault in his eyes. God
decided in advance to adopt us into his own family by
bringing us to himself through Jesus Christ. This is what
he wanted to do, and it gave him great pleasure.
(Ephesians 1:4–5 NLT)

God didn't have to rescue us. *He wanted to.* And it gave Him great pleasure to do so. This means that as much, as very much, as I long to see my kids repent and believe in Jesus Christ as their Savior, I can have peace in the assurance that God wants this for them even more.

> God didn't have to rescue us. *He wanted to.* And it gave Him great pleasure to do so.

It's no small thing that God does not want a single one of us to perish.

I have the honor and responsibility of guiding my children in truth and teaching them that Jesus is the way, the truth, the life, and the only way to the Father (John 14:6)—but I can't make them believe it. Only God can work in their hearts.

I can lay that down, and trust God with the children He's
entrusted to me.

My Child's Faith

The pressure I felt didn't end at ensuring my children's salvation. I also felt the pressure to produce in my kids a thriving and vibrant relationship with Christ once they were saved.

But I am set free from the pressure when I turn to God's Word and remember what Paul wrote to the Hebrews in Hebrews 12:2 (NIV):

> *Let us keep looking to Jesus, the author and perfecter of our faith, who for the joy set before Him endured the cross, scorning its shame, and sat down at the right hand of the throne of God.*

This means that Jesus—who is seated at the right hand of the throne of God!—is not only the originator and the creator of my child's faith, but He is the One who will grow it and see it to completion.

I can't produce a thriving faith in my kids' lives, but I can partner with God by planting "seeds of faith" in their hearts. Paul speaks to this in 1 Corinthians:

> *I planted the seed, Apollos watered it, but God has been making it grow. So neither the one who plants nor the one who waters is anything, but only God, who makes things grow.*
> (3:6–7 NIV)

See what Paul says: we *do* have a role to play in our children's lives—planting and watering—but only God "makes things grow." Through praying together, reading God's Word, memorizing Scripture, serving together, and worshipping in community, we can nurture their faith. In fact, in my previous book, *Parenting the Wholehearted Child*, I commit an entire chapter to each of these "seeds," showing how we can incorporate them practically and purposefully into our everyday lives to nurture our child's faith. But I have to remember that I don't control when and what those seeds produce. God does.

I can lay that down, and trust God with the children He's entrusted to me.

My Child's Character

And then I also felt the pressure to produce Christ-like character in my kids' lives. I believed that the only way my children would be thankful, respectful, kind, loving, honest adults was if I made sure I modeled all the right behavior and made all the right charts and had all the right jellybean obedience jars and followed all the right advice.

But I am set free from the pressure when I turn to God's Word and remember what Paul writes in Philippians 1:6, 9–11 (NLT):

I am certain that God, who began the good work within you, will continue his work until it is finally finished on the day when Christ Jesus returns. . . . I pray that your love will overflow more and more, and that you will keep on growing in knowledge and understanding. For I want you to understand what really matters, so that you may live pure and blameless lives until the day of Christ's return. May you always be filled with the fruit of your salvation—the righteous character produced in your life by Jesus Christ—for this will bring much glory and praise to God.

There is a lot packed into these four verses and I don't want us to miss a word of it.

First, we are given the assurance that it is God—not us—who began a good work within our kids. *Second,* it is God, not us, who will continue that work in their lives. And *third,* He will not give up on them even when they deserve to be given up on. He will see His work through until it is finally finished on the day when Christ Jesus returns.

The righteous character we so desperately want to see in their lives will ultimately be the fruit of their salvation, not our hard work and handmade charts. It will be produced by Jesus Christ, not by our persistence. This doesn't mean that our efforts are unimportant. Of course, they're important! But we can't anchor our hope in them. Part of God's purpose is to produce character in the lives of His children. And all of this will bring much glory and praise—not to our parenting—but to God!

Another verse that brings me great relief is Isaiah 64:8 (NIV):

> *You, Lord, are our Father. We are the clay, you are the potter. We are all the work of your hand.*

This means that the Lord, their good Father, is the actual potter of my children's lives. God, not I, sits on the potter's stool. Just as clay is dependent upon the potter to be shaped, so are we dependent upon God to shape us into the likeness of His Son.

> Just as clay is dependent upon the potter to be shaped, so are we dependent upon God to shape us into the likeness of His Son.

He does the real shaping. He does the real molding. My children (and I) are the clay in *His* skillful, faithful, and trustworthy hands. And finally, Philippians 2:13 (NLT):

> *For God is working in you, giving you the desire*
> *and the power to do what pleases him.*

I can confidently anchor my hope in the truth that God is *already* doing what He wants done in my children, and He isn't depending on me to be the Holy Spirit for them. He is the One helping them obey Him. In fact, His grace is what gives them the desire to obey Him; and by His Holy Spirit, He equips them with the power to obey Him.

I can model for them the freedom and joy that comes from obeying God's Word, but I can't make them want it. I can model life in Christ to the best of my ability, and I can use Scripture to teach my children that God's law is holy, righteous, and good (Romans 7:12) and that it is perfect, trustworthy, and more precious than gold (Psalm 19:7–10); but righteous character is produced by Jesus.

I can lay that down, and trust God with the children He's entrusted to me.

My Child's Future

I also felt the pressure to secure a hope-filled future for my kids. The pressure starts early with this one, and I know you know this pressure well.

Securing a hope-filled future begins with getting them on the correct sleeping and eating schedules right out of the gate. It means pureeing organic food so their bodies and brains thrive. It means going to the right preschool so they'll have an edge academically. It means making sure they get the best education and compete on the best teams so they can get into the best college so they can get the best job and meet the best spouse and have the best kids and own the best dog and build the best picket fence.

Kidding, not kidding.

I am certainly not condemning the desire to ensure that our kids have access to excellent opportunities and are put in good positions to utilize their gifts. I'm all for it. I am simply highlighting how much of their future I thought was dependent on how well I mapped it out.

But I am set free from the pressure when I turn to God's Word and remember what the Lord says through Jeremiah and through Paul in Ephesians.

> *I know what I'm doing. I have it all planned out—plans to take care of you, not abandon you, plans to give you the future you hope for.*
> (Jeremiah 29:11 MSG)

> *For [they] are God's masterpiece. He has created [them] anew in Christ Jesus, so [they] can do the good things he planned for [them] long ago.*
> (Ephesians 2:10 NLT)

This means that I don't have to know exactly what I'm doing because God does. God is the One who holds their future. In fact, He holds it in the very palm of His hands.

> I don't have to know exactly what I'm doing because God already does.

What I *can* do is teach them that they are each God's masterpiece, created on purpose for a purpose; and I can lead each of them in discovering God's vision for their one unique life. And as I do, I get to help them keep this important question in the forefront of their minds: *How can I use all of these God-given gifts and opportunities to advance His love and kingdom in this world?*

But God is the One who will lead my children to, and in, the very good purpose for which He created them, to do the very good things He planned since the beginning.

I can lay that down, and trust God with the children He's entrusted to me.

My Child's Happiness

I also felt the pressure to ensure my children's happiness and protect them from life's *hardships*. (Can we be real about this? It's so hard to watch our kids navigate the "gift" of hardship, even though we absolutely know that it's essential to their growing into responsible and resilient kids.) For example, I may have recently found myself tiptoeing toward trying to rescue my son from a hardship he needed to endure, when my wise hubby gently but firmly said, "Wifey, unless you plan on living in his dorm room in college and going on his honeymoon when he gets married, you need to stay out of the way and allow him to grow and trust God to use this for his good." He's a smart one, that man of mine.

It's when hardship leads to serious suffering that I *really* cling to God's Word. I find immeasurable comfort when I remember that Jesus isn't surprised or overwhelmed by their suffering. In fact, what we find in John 16:33 (NLT) is that Jesus not only told us we would experience suffering, but He assured us He has already overcome our sorrows. He says: "I have told you all this so that you may have peace in me. Here on earth you will have many trials and sorrows. But take heart, because I have overcome the world."

Suffering is a tender topic and one with which I, and I'm confident you, are well acquainted. And while we cannot eliminate our child's suffering, we can find extraordinary peace in Scripture that assures us that our suffering does not have the final word—and that all of this heartache and hurt will ultimately produce a hope that will not disappoint and a sharing in the glory of Christ.

> Suffering does not have the final word.

We find this assurance in Paul's writing on suffering in the book of Romans. In Romans 5 Paul writes:

We can rejoice, too, when we run into problems and trials, for we know that they help us develop endurance. And endurance develops strength of character, and character strengthens our confident hope of salvation. And this hope will not lead to disappointment. For we know how dearly God loves us, because he has given us the Holy Spirit to fill our hearts with his love.

(5:3–5 NLT)

Note the progression here: suffering → perseverance → character → hope. Notice that Paul says we can "rejoice" *in*—not because of, but in—our problems and trials because of what they produce in us: a hope anchored in how very much we can trust that God loves us and is for us, even in our suffering.

In Romans 8, Paul continues,

> *The Spirit himself testifies with our spirit that we are God's*
> *children. Now if we are children, then we are heirs—*
> *heirs of God and co-heirs with Christ, if indeed we share*
> *in his sufferings in order that we may also share in his*
> *glory. I consider that our present sufferings are not worth*
> *comparing with the glory that will be revealed in us.*
> (8:16–17 NIV)

A beautiful part of this verse that I've missed for most of my life is this: *We are heirs of God and co-heirs with Christ.* That's an extraordinary inheritance! But as co-heirs, we will share in His suffering just as we will share in His glory. They go hand in hand.

When pain and suffering come knocking, we should not be surprised (see 1 Peter 4:12). While it hurts like all get-out to watch our children hurt, we must hold on to God's Word. It's our only hope. We have to know that as co-heirs with Christ, their suffering cannot hold a candle to the glory—and the *incomparable* happiness—that is awaiting them and that will be revealed in them.

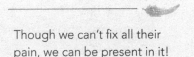

Though we can't fix all their pain, we can be present in it!

And though we can't fix all their pain, we can be present in it! When our kids are hurting, crushed, or confused, they need parents who are willing to lean into their pain, listen without lecturing, and love without limits.

I can lay that down, and trust God with the children He's entrusted to me.

It All Belongs to God

We could do this all day. We could walk through verse after verse that reveals God's grace and sovereignty over the things we worry most about. Are you catching a glimpse of just how good this Good News is? The things we feel pressured to produce in our children's lives are ultimately *all* the work of the Father, the Son, and the Holy Spirit. It all belongs to Him:

- He woos them to Himself and calls them to salvation.
- He authors and perfects their faith.
- He gives them the desire and power to do what pleases Him, producing righteous character in their lives.
- He has their hope-filled future all planned out.
- He allows them to share in His suffering that they may also share in His glory.

Our children were *God's* good idea to begin with. They are His workmanship.

Again, this is not to suggest that God is making our children's choices. Our children, like us, have human free will. Still, it gives me immeasurable hope to remember that

48

God loves our children and longs for them even more than we do! Let's not forget, our children were *His* good idea to begin with. Your son. Your daughter. They were God's good idea. They are His workmanship. And His heart belongs to them. So we can lay our burdens down and trust Him with the children He has entrusted to us.

Now, before it sounds like I'm inviting us to throw in the towel, kick up our feet, and do a lot of nothing while God does everything, let's turn now to the next two chapters, where we will explore what God's Word says about the significance of our role in our children's lives. In fact, we can't read this chapter without reading the next, or we will have only half the story. If we stop now, we miss out on the profound ways God wants to use us and partner with us in the lives of our kids. And it just keeps getting better.

CHAPTER 5

The Freedom to Rely on the Power of Prayer

and Experience God's Peace in Our Hearts

Most mornings when I come downstairs, I find a copy of Jodie Berndt's book, *Praying the Scriptures for Your Children* opened up and facedown on the kitchen counter, alongside an empty cup of coffee. I know, on these mornings, that my husband spent a few moments praying for our kids before taking off for work. He is long gone before the boys and I make our ways to the kitchen, but oh, how I love the book on the counter that ever so gently says to our boys, "Your earthly father has been hanging out with your heavenly Father, praying very specifically about each one of you!"

It has never ceased to amaze us how the things we go to bed wrestling with (and worried about!) have been the very things Jodie Berndt's book has addressed in Scripture during Mike's prayer time the next morning. It's God's kindness (and sense of humor, I suppose) to meet us in His Word and say, "Hey, that thing you're worried about. I just want to remind you, I know and I've got it!"

Pray about Everything

We've just spent an entire chapter exploring all of the things we *can't* do, right? So I wouldn't be surprised if now you're thinking, *After all that talk about what I can't do, please tell me what I* can!

I hear you! So let's start with what I believe is the most powerful thing, and that is prayer.

Our prayers have a profound impact on our kids' lives.

Friend, we do our best parenting through prayer!

We do our best parenting through prayer.

Now maybe you already know that. Maybe you already know how powerful prayer is, and yet, like me, your prayer life doesn't always reflect that truth. You know what I mean? So nobody needs to be reminded of this more than I do, because too often my life suggests that we do our best parenting—not through prayer—but through worry.

Worry. This is one of those things we mommas do well. We worry about our kids—the decisions they make and the hardships they face. We worry about most of the parenting decisions we make and whether we've got it right. We do this, even though we know, in the words of Corrie ten Boom, that "worry does not empty tomorrow of its sorrow. It empties today of its strength."

And, if you're anything like me, you do your "best" worrying around three in the morning. Nothing like trying to be a good mom after a good long night of sleepless worry.

But what if, instead of worrying, we heeded Paul's instruction? He writes:

> *Don't worry about anything; instead, pray about*
> *everything. Tell God what you need, and thank him for*
> *all he has done. Then you will experience God's peace,*
> *which exceeds anything we can understand. His peace will*
> *guard your hearts and minds as you live in Christ Jesus.*
> (Philippians 4:6–7 NLT)

Paul says, "Instead of worrying, pray!" Take it all—every last bit of it—to God. He doesn't say, "Pray about some things." He says, "Pray about everything."

And when we do, Paul assures, we will experience the peace our hearts crave.

The peace our hearts crave *in the midst of all the pressure*— the peace that "exceeds anything we can understand"—can be found in only one place. And it isn't in problem solving. It's in prayer.

Paul doesn't only encourage us to pray about "everything." He encourages us to do it "continually." He writes in 1 Thessalonians 5:16–18 (NIV), "Rejoice always, pray continually, give thanks in all circumstances; for this is God's will for you in Christ Jesus."

Have you ever asked, "What is God's will? I just want to know what God's will is in this situation or circumstance!" Well,

Paul's instruction above is a great place to start. In fact, what if we committed to shaping every worry we carry into prayer and thanksgiving?

Now notice, this verse doesn't say "give thanks *for* all your circumstances." Paul isn't saying that God's will for you is to be thankful for tragedy and turmoil in your child's life. But He is showing us how we can remain thankful for who Jesus is and what Jesus can do "*in* all circumstances."

So, what if, every time a worry tried to settle in our souls, we walked in God's will and gave it back to God in prayer and gave thanks *in* our circumstances. I can only imagine the impact.

I'm feeling super convicted as I write this to you. Because, truth be told, I am doing a whole lot of worrying for my children right now. I'm worrying about a child who is being targeted by a peer, a child who is not motivated to fulfill his God-given purpose and potential, a child who doesn't see the harm in little white lies, a child who gets too angry too easily, a child who is having horrible dreams and sleepless nights. I won't keep going because I know you have enough worries of your own—but goodness, do I worry. I worry mostly because it hurts to see our kids struggle, but also because I struggle to know what to do.

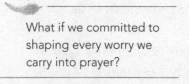

What if we committed to shaping every worry we carry into prayer?

Thankfully, James, the brother of Jesus, has good words for us about our struggle.

He writes, "If you don't know what you're doing, pray to the Father. He loves to help" (James 1:5 MSG).

Okay, my fellow mom. How often do you feel like you don't

know what you're doing as a parent? Or better said, how often do you feel like you have *no living clue* what you're doing? James tells us to pray to our all-knowing, all-loving heavenly Father who loves to help.

Then James goes on to write, "You'll get his help, and won't be condescended to when you ask for it. Ask boldly, believingly, without a second thought" (James 1:6 MSG).

We are invited to bring all our uncertainty and all our inadequacy to our Father who *loves* to help. And God's Word assures us that we can have peace amidst the pressure.

> God's Word assures us that we can have peace amidst the pressure.

So what in the world are we doing settling for anything less than that?

Partner with God through Prayer

Prayer is not only the antidote to finding peace amidst all of the pressure, but it is our most powerful weapon against the enemy who, like it or not, is working against us. He "prowls around like a roaring lion looking for someone to devour" (1 Peter 5:8 NIV). I don't say this to scare us. I say this to encourage us to get on our knees and fight for our kids in prayer.

Our prayers for our children (and with our children!) are unimaginably significant. Through prayer, we get to partner with God in the work He is doing in the lives of our kids, all the while remembering that "It won't be long before this generous God who has great plans for us in Christ—eternal and glorious plans they are!—will have you put together and on your feet for good. He gets the last word; yes, He does!" (1 Peter 5:11 MSG).

In other words, as we pray for our kids, we can trust that God—who is abundantly generous—has great plans for our kids in Christ. And not just temporal plans, but eternal plans. And He gets the last word—*yes, He does!* We can rest in His sovereignty and surrender to His will, just as we see Jesus surrendering to His Father's will in His prayer at Gethsemane. Jesus models prayer for us.

In the Gospel of Mark, chapter 14, we find that Jesus is "overwhelmed with sorrow to the point of death" (v. 34 NIV). Jesus knew that the fulfillment of His mission was imminent. He would soon take on the sin of the world and bear the wrath and shame for the entire human race. Jesus was "deeply distressed and troubled" when He prayed, "Abba Father, everything is possible for you. Take this cup from me. Yet not what I will, but what you will" (v. 36 NIV).

> We can pray for our children like Jesus prayed to His Father: "I know you can. I pray you would. Your will be done."

When our hearts are aching and our fears are raging, we can pray for our children like Jesus prayed to His Father: "I know you can. I pray you would. Your will be done."[1] This simple but profound prayer guides us in acknowledging God's power, submitting to His will, and trusting in His goodness.

When You Don't Know How or What to Pray

The above prayer has expanded my heart and opened my hands to God's perfect will in times when I have come to Him very fearful and close-fisted. Maybe you, too, sometimes come before God fearful and close-fisted? Or maybe you're a mom who doesn't know how to pray or what to say. Or perhaps you're in a season where you feel particularly helpless or hopeless. Or maybe words fail you because you are so overwhelmed and under pressure that you don't even know where to begin. Or you're worried that your doubts or lack of faith will hinder your prayers for your children. If so, may I encourage you in your prayer life. Paul writes:

> *God's Spirit is right alongside helping us along. If we don't know how or what to pray, it doesn't matter. He does our praying in and for us, making prayer out of our wordless sighs, our aching groans. He knows us far better than we know ourselves, knows our pregnant condition, and keeps us present before God. That's why we can be so sure that every detail in our lives of love for God is worked into something good.*
> (Romans 8:26–28 MSG)

The assurance Paul gives us in Romans 8 is that God's very Spirit—who knows us better than we know ourselves—takes our cries for help and does our praying in and for us. That's incredible. Be honest with Him. Share your heart with Him. You don't have to know exactly what to say or how to say it. He isn't judging or critiquing your prayers. Nobody listens better than Jesus.

Nobody listens better than Jesus.

You can even ask God to help you overcome your unbelief. You don't have to hide your doubts and disbelief from God. (He already knows them, by the way.)

We see this so beautifully demonstrated in the gospel of Mark, chapter 9, when a father brought his sick son to Jesus for healing. He said,

> *"Have mercy on us and help us, if you can." And Jesus replied, "What do you mean, 'If I can'? Anything is possible if a person believes." Then the father instantly cried out, "I do believe, but help me overcome my unbelief!"*
> (vv. 22–24 NLT)

Like the father of the sick son, we can ask Jesus, the author and perfecter of our faith (Hebrews 12:2), to help us overcome our doubts and believe that anything is possible with God.

Are we seeing how profound our prayers are in our parenting and in the lives of our children? Now, this is not discounting the fact that there are very real things we must do and very difficult problems we must solve. Nowhere in Scripture do we read, "Pray *only*." Right? But we are continually reminded that this is the best place to start and the best place to return! As we navigate each one of the pressures we've covered, and we do the things God has called us to do as parents, we can do it with open hands and trusting hearts—believing that God is sovereign, that He is good, and that there is grace upon grace for us and for our kids.

But before we move on, I want to encourage you with one

of my most treasured passages in all of Scripture. In 1 Peter 5:7, the apostle Peter writes, "Cast all your anxiety on Him because He cares for you" (1 Peter 5:7 NIV). Our heavenly Father cares so deeply for us that He wants us to surrender the burdens and worries and anxiety that we are carrying to Him. He wants us to let Him carry it for us in His strong arms of grace.

So before we turn the page, can we take a moment and do just that? Let's do some casting. It's time to walk lighter and breathe deeper.

CHAPTER 6

The Freedom to Make the Gospel Central in Our Parenting

and Experience God's Grace in Our Homes

can't think of a better place to for us to start our conversa-tion about the significant role we play in our children's lives than with Deuteronomy 6:4–7. If we want to know what God has called us to do, we can find the answer here. This is one of the *linchpin* scriptures of the whole Bible—a scripture that, accord-ing to Jesus, is the summation of *all* the law and *all* the prophets. And it holds great guidance for us as parents.

In this passage we find Moses instructing the Israelite people on what to do with the Ten Commandments he's just given them. He says:

> *Hear, O Israel: The Lord our God, the Lord is one. Love the Lord your God with all your heart and with all your soul and with all your strength. These commandments that I give you*

today are to be on your hearts. Impress them on your children.
Talk about them when you sit at home and when you walk
along the road, when you lie down and when you get up.
(Deuteronomy 6:4–7 NIV)

Now, to fully appreciate all that God is saying to us through Moses, we can't miss the very first line of this passage: *"The Lord our God, the Lord is one."* This proclamation assures us of what we've just explored: because God is sovereign, we can live and parent with confident assurance in His absolute authority over *all* things. This assurance of God's sovereignty wasn't just for Israel back then. It's for us, right now. It's a reminder that amid our daily tribulation and chaos, serenity and peace of heart are available to us to the extent that we trust in God.

> Amid our daily tribulation and chaos, serenity and peace of heart are available to us to the extent that we trust in God.

After affirming God's sovereignty, Moses affirms our significant role. He says we are called to love God with our whole being. And *then* we are called to impress on our kids a whole-being love for God and nurture that love on a daily basis.

Later, in the New Testament, Jesus echoes Moses' powerful declaration that we are to love God foremost.

A proud religious law-keeper who knew the Law tried to
trap Jesus. He said, "Teacher, which one is the greatest of
the Laws?" Jesus said to him, " 'You must love the Lord
your God with all your heart and with all your soul and
with all your mind. This is the first and greatest of the Laws.

The second is like it: You must love your neighbor as you love yourself.' All the Laws and the writings of the early preachers depend on these two most important Laws."
(Matthew 22:35–40 NIV)

Seeking to raise a child who loves the Lord with all his heart, soul, and mind is our highest calling as parents.

Now, if you're thinking, "This is no small task! This is a lot of pressure!" I get it. But with the commission comes the grace. His grace is the motivating and empowering fuel.

To demonstrate what I mean, I want us to take a quick look at Deuteronomy 5—the chapter prior to our linchpin passage—and notice what God says *just before* he gave Moses the Ten Commandments. He says, "I am the Lord your God, who brought you out of the land of Egypt, out of the house of slavery" (5:6 NIV). *Then* He gives the Ten Commandments.

Do you see what God is doing? Before He commands them to love and obey, He first reminds His people of His nature, of His character, and of His rescuing grace. In other words, He is showing how His redeeming love was not predicated on their love and obedience. He rescued them *first.*

God is declaring the Gospel message—a message that is woven throughout all of Scripture and that we will see throughout the rest of our time together. God's grace is not contingent on our performance and obedience. And only grace can motivate and enable loving obedience to God.

God's love for us stimulates our love for Him, and our love for God stimulates obedience.

We see this truth reinforced in countless passages in Scripture, but I love how simply—but profoundly—John frames this in 1 John 4:19 (NIV). He writes: "We love because He first loved us."

In other words, our love for God is our grateful response to the love God has given us in the sacrifice of His Son. God's love inspires ours.

Impressing God's Love on Our Kids

What does this Gospel message have to do with our parenting? Everything! Because herein we discover how to fulfill our calling: we impress on our kids a whole-being love for God by first impressing on our kids God's indescribable love for them.

> We impress on our kids a love for God by first impressing on our kids God's love for them.

See, our kids need to know God's heart *for them* before they will ever desire to seek His heart above all else! They need to know the extent to which God went to rescue them and demonstrate His love for them in the life, death, and resurrection of Jesus Christ (2 Corinthians 5:21).

If we try to raise kids who love God only by giving them the commandments of God and telling them they *should* love God, we will more likely raise rule followers than God lovers. We'll more likely raise kids who flee the faith because rules don't breed gratitude and melt our hearts. Love does.

Think about it. We know this to be true in our own lives. We want to follow God to the extent that we have experienced— personally tasted—the extravagance of His grace for us. The real us. The sinful, flawed, broken, imperfect us. It's not the "shoulds" and "oughts" that build love for God. It's that He loved us enough to rescue us, even while we were running and rebelling and refusing to love Him in return.

When we are personally "impressed" with the extent of God's love, then we will *want to*—not *have to*—love God. And this is what we most need to remember when leading our kids in loving and serving God and one another—*we love because He first loved us.*

This is the Gospel—the Good News of Jesus Christ that transforms hearts and homes!

The Gospel Inspires Love for God

Now, "The Gospel" is one of those expressions that I've heard for as long as I can remember, but I never fully understood what it *really* meant. So, just in case you've wondered the same thing, I thought we might take a moment to unpack it.

- The Gospel is the Good News that "Christ Jesus came into the world to save sinners" (1 Timothy 1:15). That Jesus Christ did for you and for me what we could never do for ourselves.
- The Gospel is the Good News that Jesus' perfect life, death, and resurrection has secured God's eternal and unwavering love for us, acceptance of us, delight in us, and pleasure over us.
- The Gospel is the Good News that when we believe in and rely on Jesus' perfect work and record (rather than our own striving and performance), we never

have to fear our Father's rejection. We can never outsin His grace. We can never lose His love.

When we believe in and rely on Jesus' perfect work and record, we never have to fear our Father's rejection.

This oh-so-Good-News about God's deep and boundless love is the foundation on which our children's love for God is built.

A recent article published by The Gospel Coalition affirmed this Gospel-centered approach to parenting. It concludes:

> The common thread that binds together almost every ministry-minded twenty-something that I know is abundantly clear: a home where the gospel was not peripheral but absolutely central.
>
> The twenty-somethings who are serving, leading, and driving the ministries at our church were kids whose parents . . . ultimately operated from a framework of grace that held up the cross of Jesus as the basis for peace with God and forgiveness toward one another.
>
> This is not a formula! Kids from wonderful gospel-centered homes leave the church; people from messed-up family backgrounds find eternal life in Jesus and have beautiful marriages and families. But it's also not a crap-shoot. In general, children who are led in their faith during their growing-up years by parents who love Jesus vibrantly, serve their church actively, and saturate their home with the gospel completely, grow up to love Jesus and the church.[1]

The common thread found in kids who live out their faith was growing up in a home where the gospel was not peripheral, but *central*.

Both a Privilege and a Responsibility

We, as moms, have the great privilege of—and responsibility to—impress upon our kids the heart-melting, life-giving news that "immense in mercy and with an incredible love, he embraced us. He took our sin-dead lives and made us alive in Christ" (Ephesians 2:4–5 MSG).

Indeed it is both a privilege *and* a responsibility. And trust me when I tell you, I'm talking to myself here because I am often convicted about how I prioritize nurturing my child's faith. I have to continually re-evaluate what I prioritize in our lives and whether I am parenting with eternity in the forefront of my mind.

You see, our culture tells us that our ultimate goal should be to launch kids who will have *big* bank accounts and *big* résumés and *big* awards and *big* toys. But Scripture paints a very different picture. Our ultimate goal should be to launch kids who have a *big* faith anchored in the *big* grace of God. Of *all* the things we can give our kids in this world, God has called us to give them Him above all else. Because only in Him will they find the fulfillment their hearts crave, and only in Him will they find the purpose-filled future He designed for them. This world is not their permanent home, and it's our job to help them live in light of eternity. Living in the grace of God for the glory of God!

Vessels of the Gospel

Now, if you're anything like me, you are ready to turn the page to find the top five things we can do today to get going on fulfilling this significant role in our kids' lives. So I want to assure you that how we make the Gospel central in our homes on a daily basis will be our focus in the third section. But first, can I share with you the most important truth God has revealed to me as a parent? If we want to impress on the hearts of our children the unending and unconditional love of God, we *first* need to know and accept the unending and unconditional love of God *for us*! If we don't accept God's grace for us in all of *our* weaknesses, sin, and failure, how can we be the vessel through which our kids experience God's grace in all of *their* weaknesses, sin, and failure?

We need to know—really know—that Jesus loves *us* and that His grace is for *us*. And we need to allow God to do in us what we ultimately long for Him to do in our children—to melt our hearts with His love and mold us more and more into His image by the power of His Holy Spirit.

> We need to allow God to do in us what we ultimately long for Him to do in our children.

So, my friend, in the next section, we are going to do some *heart* work. And it sometimes might feel like *hard* work. But it will be so very worth it!

We will identify those things that keep us from believing we are *already* lovable to our Father and discover fresh truth about God's unwavering acceptance of us. We will shed our shame and leave behind the lies that are preventing us from living in freedom. We will lose the labels that we've allowed to define us, and we will beg the Holy Spirit to open the eyes of our hearts to our true identities—identities that are firmly anchored in being God's beloved. And we will stop striving to "be enough" because we will know with certainty that Christ *in us* is enough.

All the pressure we've been carrying—the pressure to be awesome for God, the pressure to be awesome for our kids, and the pressure to raise awesome kids—we can lay it all down.

Our role is to give the grace and truth of Christ *to* our children—not to be the perfection and provision of Christ *for* our children. Are you ready to live like that's true? I could not wait for us to get to this part. I know we're prone to looking for a straight line to tested formulas for being better moms raising better kids, but trust me. The straight line's got nothing on where we're headed. Let's turn the page with the great expectation that God is about to transform our own hearts with His wild love and free us to live—and parent—in the fullness of His grace!

PART TWO

Living in Grace

CHAPTER 7

Our Struggle: A Little More Perfect = a Little More Lovable

God's Truth: Because of Jesus, God Can't Stop Loving Me

Our three older boys share one bedroom. They've done this for years, by choice. As long and as hard as the day can be between three boys who span only five years in age, they still love being together at the end of the day, and for that I'm incredibly grateful. It sure did simplify the bedtime routine in their early years. Not to mention that it gave us a ready and waiting bedroom when our little guy was born almost seven years later.

Each evening, once all three boys are snuggled into their beds, we aim to read the Bible together. The key word here is *aim*. And in the spirit of keeping it real, let me assure you it does not happen every night. Let me also assure you, we don't do this because we fancy ourselves as a good and holy family. No. We do it because we know how desperately we need to daily draw close to the Good News of our good and holy God at the end of our crazy days.

On one particular evening it was Owen's turn to choose the Bible story. He opened up his *Jesus Storybook Bible* and decided to go all the way back to the beginning. He chose the creation story. We read about how God created everything out of nothing, and we read how God simply spoke, and whatever He said happened.

When Owen was done reading, I asked, "Wow, boys! If God can do that, is there anything He can't do?"

To my surprise my son Brennan exclaimed, "Yeah, Mom. There is something He can't do!"

I'm not gonna lie, I was a little worried. *How have we gotten this wrong*? I wondered.

But before the train went completely off the tracks, Brennan continued. "Mom, God can't stop loving us! That's what He can't do!"

From the mouths of babes, right?

God Can't Stop Loving Us

When we are in Christ, God can't stop loving us! The real us. The rebellious us. The unfaithful us. But, believing that can be so hard! Why? Well, for starters, there are simply too many parts of us that feel too unlovable. I know you know what I'm talking about. We know the mess that lies beneath our well-manicured outsides. Also, let's not negate the power of the persistent message our culture bombards us with: "A little more perfect = a little more lovable." Everywhere we turn, covert and overt messages assure us that our lovability is riding on our performance.

Then we go a step further and apply that equation to our relationship with our heavenly Father, and we think, *The better I can be for God, the more I will be loved and accepted by God.*

In other words, we forget (or doubt) what the Word of God says about the love of God. Or maybe

> Our culture bombards us with a persistent message: a little more perfect = a little more lovable.

it's that we simply assume we are exempt from God's promises in passages such as these:

> *For his unfailing love toward those who fear him is*
> *as great as the height of the heavens above the earth.*
> *He has removed our sins as far from us as the east is*
> *from the west. The Lord is like a father to his children,*
> *tender and compassionate to those who fear him.*
> (Psalm 103:11–13 NLT)

> *Yet hope returns when I remember this one thing:*
> *The Lord's unfailing love and mercy still continue,*
> *fresh as the morning, as sure as the sunrise. The Lord*
> *is all I have, and so in him I put my hope.*
> (Lamentations 3:21–24 GNT)

> *I have loved you, My people, with an everlasting love.*
> *With unfailing love I have drawn you to Myself!*
> (Jeremiah 31:3 NLT)

And these three verses only scratch the surface. God couldn't be clearer. His love is not reliant on our lovability. Because of Jesus, it remains unfailing amidst all of our failures.

If you're anything like me, however, you might read those verses and say with your mouth, "I know God will always love me." But the way you live your life—ceaselessly trying harder to be a "better Christian" so you can earn or keep His love—tells a different story.

"Earning My Keep"

In spite of what God's Word tells us, I have spent the majority of my life trying to make it easier for God to love me and "keep" his grace going for me. Which is ironic, really, because I was a preacher's kid, raised in a very grace-filled home. So when God saved me when I was eight years old, I understood, as much as an eight-year-old can, that "it is by grace you have been saved, through faith—and this is not from yourselves, it is the gift of God—not by works, so that no one can boast" (Ephesians 2:8–9 NIV).

> What I struggled to accept is that God's grace was not only for my salvation but also for my ongoing sin and weakness.

Yes, I knew that God's grace was for my salvation. But, what I struggled to accept, as I got older and my sinful nature was more exposed, is that God's grace is also for my *ongoing* sin and weakness. Said differently, the more aware I became of just how short I fall of the glory of God (Romans 3:23), the more pressure I felt to attain unachievable perfection—to both keep God happy and to be a good "witness."

In my efforts to "earn my keep," I lived under a banner of the three deadly *P* words. Those three pressure-inducing and joy-stealing words are *perfection*, *performance*, and *pretension*. See if any of these messages feel familiar to you.

Perfection: Strive for flawlessness. Don't dare fall short of those excessively high expectations you have of yourself, lest you become less lovable. The more perfect you are, the more acceptable you are to God.

Performance: You are what you do. So do a lot to prove you are worth a lot. Play all the roles well and whatever you do, don't let them see you struggle. Others' applause and admiration hinges on your ability to pull this off.

Pretension: Wear a mask of the more likable version of yourself and hide the real you. Better yet, try to be someone else. The real you isn't enough. The real you—the you who is far more insecure, far more jealous, far more fearful, far more exhausted, far more angry, and far more unsatisfied than you'd ever want others to discover—isn't that lovable after all.

That's the banner I lived under, as though there were a follow-up verse to Ephesians 2:8–9 that reads: "... However, it is by your hard work and ceaseless striving that you will remain loved and accepted. You can't save yourself. That is my doing. But you can try really hard to keep me happy and not lose my affection. It's the least you can do, really, for all that I've done for you."

> There is no passage in Scripture that says: "Jesus' job was to save you. Your job is to keep God happy." I just lived like there was.

But of course that verse is nowhere to be found in Scripture. There is no such follow-up verse in Ephesians that says, "Jesus' job was to save you. Your job is to keep God happy." I just lived like there was. I thought God's love was something we work hard to keep and work hard to earn back when it's lost.

Declared Righteous in Christ!

What Scripture *does* say, however, is that "God made him who had no sin to be sin for us, so that in him we might become the righteousness of God" (2 Corinthians 5:21 NIV).

Meaning, when we are in Christ, we *are declared righteous.* We are head-to-toe, inside-and-out, *covered* in the perfection of Jesus Christ. Made right with God, even while we are yet sinners. So we can stop striving for a seal of approval that has already been given to us by God in Jesus Christ.

> We can stop striving for a seal of approval that has already been given to us by God in Jesus Christ.

This means that the perfection I'd been ceaselessly striving for my whole life, in order to feel worthy of God's love and grace, was already all mine, all because Jesus says, "I have her covered!" I was free to stop pursuing perfection and to start pursuing the person of Christ.

God created us to *thrive* in the unwavering assurance of His love, which is given to us because of Jesus. But instead of thriving in God's love, most of us are doing something radically different. We are *striving*. Striving for something that is actually already all ours! And here's the thing: Oftentimes we don't even realize we are living this way.

Awakening to Grace

If you know Jesus, you know there is so much *joy* in Him. But my family and I tasted so little of it because I was striving to achieve a righteousness of my own, and *I was putting that same pressure on my kids.* Because I was trying to keep God's love through my good behavior, I also raised my three young boys through that lens.

Grace, real grace, was lost on me. Or maybe it's just that I settled for grace with strings attached—which isn't really grace at all. And that is really what I want us to get to the bottom of, because I believe that is where most of us get stuck.

See, for years I strove (and I mean *strove*) to be a better mom. There wasn't a book or a blog I didn't read about how to be a grace-full mom who raises great and godly kids. But no matter how hard I tried, I kept failing to give grace and show grace to my kids.

From the outside, it may have looked like I was pulling it off. But on the inside, I was desperate, overwhelmed, ashamed, and hopeless—because I was realizing how incapable I was of being the perfect Christian woman and wife and mom I'd set out to be.

I was a coming-undone mother to three boys under five, who ended most nights in tears on the couch over my parenting failures, when I had what I only know to describe as an awakening to the gospel.

The couch on which I cried tears of shame became the couch on which I profoundly experienced God's grace. It was an ordinary evening. I was reading my Bible to complete homework for a Bible study I was doing with a group of girlfriends, and the study guided me to Ephesians, chapter 3—a chapter I'd read countless times throughout my life. But on this particular evening, God used this passage to speak directly to my heart. That moment was the beginning of God slowly but surely opening the eyes of my heart to His unrelenting love for me in Jesus Christ—just as I was—and I was never the same.

I fell in love with Jesus all over again, and I began to devour books by authors who wrote about the profound depth of God's grace. In doing so, I discovered that the Bible's primary function isn't to serve as an instruction manual telling us how to be perfect, as I'd always assumed. The Bible, to borrow the words of the apostle Paul, testifies to the Gospel of the grace of God (Acts 20:24).

> The Bible's primary function isn't to serve as an instruction manual telling us how to be perfect. The Bible testifies to the Gospel of the grace of God.

As God began opening the eyes of my heart to His grace, everything began to change radically. I became free to confess that I am a great sinner who has a greater Savior. I was free to lighten up and let joy live loud in our home.

What I now wanted to do was raise kids who not only knew the importance of obeying God's *law* but kids who also, first and foremost, knew the magnitude of God's *grace*. Kids who knew how wide and how long and how high and how deep God's love is in Jesus Christ (Ephesians 3:17–19).

How Would Your Parenting Look, If...

Friend, can we pause here and ask ourselves a couple of questions? Big questions. The kind that can potentially change our lives in a radical way: How would your life—and your parenting—be different if you *really* believed and lived from the truth that God can't stop loving you, just as you are, not as you wish you were?

What burdens would you lay down?

What shame would you shed?

What freedom would you walk in?

From what striving would you cease if you truly believed that God's inexhaustible grace is not only for your salvation but also for your ongoing sanctification?

Sanctification is the ongoing process by which we grow more and more into the likeness of Christ—as we rely more and more on the transforming power of Christ. It is not "look how hard I'm trying and how much better I'm getting and how much less I need grace." By *His* grace and the power of *His* Spirit, God delights to craft us more into His image for our joy and for His glory. And He never, ever, gives up on us.

With that understanding of sanctification in mind, will you just sit with these questions for a moment? Be honest with yourself. Be honest with God. Maybe even invite Him to open up your heart to the magnitude of His love for you.

Coming to believe that God can't stop loving you can bring the greatest transformation your life has ever known. And this transformation will—it can't not—overflow into your parenting. That is precisely why this discussion is so im-

> Becoming more the moms we long to be happens by coming to believe the Gospel more deeply for ourselves.

portant. Becoming more the moms we long to be happens by coming to believe the Gospel more deeply for ourselves!

Discovering Grace Alongside Our Kids

If accepting God's unconditional love for you is something you struggle with, or if this whole idea of seeing yourself as a beloved child of God is foreign to you, please don't despair. You're not alone. I'm still learning *each and every day* how to surrender to God's grace. Living in grace continues to be a daily surrender to the Holy Spirit's work in my life as I stumble through this parenting thing—and through this life-in-general thing.

Believing we are unconditionally loved by God is not something we must have "mastered" in order to lead our children in it. The mystery of grace can't be mastered. We can, however, discover and receive and enjoy God's grace *alongside* our kids! Alongside. In fact, the older I get, the more aware I become of just how much I still have to discover about God's grace and how much God uses my kids to teach me about His grace. This is a journey, and we are all on it. And while the finish line isn't on this side of heaven, grace will lead us all the way home.

CHAPTER 8

Our Struggle: My Sin Is Too Great

God's Truth: God's Grace Is Greater

I think it's safe to say that the apostle Paul penned the cry of many mothers' hearts when he wrote Romans, chapter 7. In fact, if Paul hadn't written this almost two thousand years ago, I'd think he snuck into my house and stole an excerpt from my journal.

Now, before we read this passage, let's remember who Paul is. This is the apostle Paul—formerly Saul, a Jewish Pharisee who hated Christians and "persecuted the church of God violently and tried to destroy it" (Galatians 1:13 ESV). But through his transforming experience with God on the Damascus road, he is now a devout follower of Christ, completely sold out for Jesus, "preaching the faith he once tried to destroy" (Galatians 1:23–24 ESV).

With this in mind, let's read what the apostle Paul writes in Romans 7:

I realize that I don't have what it takes. I can will it, but I can't do it. I decide to do good, but I don't really do it; I decide not to do bad, but then I do it anyway. My decisions, such as they are, don't result in actions. Something has gone wrong deep within me and gets the better of me every time. It happens so regularly that it's predictable. The moment I decide to do good, sin is there to trip me up. I truly delight in God's commands, but it's pretty obvious that not all of me joins in that delight. Parts of me covertly rebel, and just when I least expect it, they take charge. I've tried everything and nothing helps. I'm at the end of my rope. Is there no one who can do anything for me? Isn't that the real question?
(Romans 7:18–24 MSG)

Maybe you've also felt some—or all—of what Paul is confessing here.

- I decide to do good, but I don't really do it; I decide not to do bad, but then I do it anyway.
- It happens so regularly that it's predictable.
- The moment I decide to do good, sin is there to trip me up.
- I truly delight in God's commands, but it's pretty obvious that not all of me joins in that delight.

Maybe you have written something like this in your own journal, or if you're really brave, you may have said something like it to a friend over coffee.

Now let's clarify what Paul is saying. He is not saying that we should just surrender to living in constant defeat because of our sin. What he *is* doing is expressing his angst over his persistently sinful nature and his inability to live in complete victory over it. His words demonstrate how even Christians who love God and love His law and desire to be free from the sting of sin still can't attain perfection in this life.

Well, we'd all be in big trouble if this were the end of Paul's writing. But instead we find good news, the best news, in Paul's response to his own question: *"Is there no one who can do anything for me?"* His answer is sweet music:

> *The answer, thank God, is that Jesus Christ can and does. He acted to set things right in this life of contradictions where I want to serve God with all my heart and mind, but am pulled by the influence of sin to do something totally different.*
> (Romans 7:25 MSG)

Did you catch that, my friend? *"The answer, thank God, is that Jesus Christ can and does."* Jesus is the answer.

Paul says something similar earlier in Romans as well:

> *For all have sinned and fall short of the glory of God, and are justified by his grace as a gift, through the redemption that is in Christ Jesus, whom God put forward as a propitiation by his blood, to be received by faith.*
> (Romans 3:23–25 ESV)

Let's not miss this!

Because of Jesus, we are justified the moment we believe—which means we are made right with God, counted righteous, even while we are still sinners.

And because of Jesus, we are forgiven and set free.

But there's even more good news! As Paul writes in Corinthians:

> *Therefore, if anyone is in Christ, he is a new creation.*
> *The old has passed away; behold, the new has come.*
> (2 Corinthians 5:17 ESV)

In other words, by Christ's work alone, we are justified, redeemed, *and* we become new creations in Christ. (And *still*, that's not the entirety of the blessings we receive in Christ, but we will soon get to the rest.)

Not Either/Or but Both/And

See, in Romans 7, Paul is painfully aware of who he is—in the flesh—in his persistently sinful nature. Yet, at the very same time, his assurance and his hope is in his identity in Christ, which is 100 percent righteous before God.

Likewise, *we* remain sinful in the Christian life *as lived*, but our identity *in Christ* is total righteousness. Our truest identity is "a new creation in Christ" (2 Corinthians 5:17). This is why Paul says, "It is no longer I myself who do it, but it is sin living in me" (Romans 7:17 NIV). See how he separates his identity as a new creation in Christ from the sin that resides within him?

It's what Martin Luther famously called, *"Simul iustus et peccator"*—we are simultaneously justified and a sinner. It's not *either/or* but *both/and*.

I'm especially grateful for how Tim Keller frames the tension
of the both/and in the Christian life.
He writes, "We are more sinful and
flawed in ourselves than we ever
dared believe, yet at the very same
time we are more loved and accepted in Jesus Christ than we ever
dared hope."[1]

> We are simultaneously justified
> and a sinner. It's not *either/or*
> but *both/and.*

I'm not sure how I missed this intoxicating truth for most of
my life. All I know is that I did. And the pressure to live in con-
tinual victory over sin was crushing me.

Maybe you can relate? Or, maybe, you lean toward the other
end of the spectrum.

Because not all moms feel "too sinful," as I did. Some of us
minimize our sin and believe we're really not all that sinful after
all. So I want to touch on that briefly.

If we think, *You know I'm not really all that bad. I mean,
sometimes I gossip and tell a white lie and drink too much wine
and drive too fast. But I don't do the really "bad stuff,"* then
we've set the bar too low. Because God's law not only requires
perfection in our outward actions but it also requires that our
hearts be pure and perfect, too. And not just some of the time,
but all of the time. And the only solution to our sin—no matter
how small or big—is the sinless life and sacrifice of Jesus Christ.
We will dig deeper into God's command for perfection in the
coming chapters, but for now, I want us to see how if we convince ourselves we are "good enough" we won't recognize our
soul-deep need for a rescuer. If we think we are loved and accepted by God *apart* from the work of Jesus, we won't see our

need *for* Jesus. And we will never truly walk in the freedom of the Cross and grow in grace.

It's only when we acknowledge who we really are *apart* from Christ—sinful, broken, prone to wander—that we will live in gratitude for who we are *in* Christ—beloved, chosen, and beautiful before our holy God.

> It's only when we acknowledge who we really are *apart* from Christ that we will live in gratitude for who we are *in* Christ.

As Brennan Manning writes: "To live by grace means to acknowledge my whole life story, the light side and the dark. In admitting my shadow side, I learn who I am and what God's grace means."[2]

In Christ, we are new creations, called not to perfection, but to the pursuit of Christ. Called to become *who we already are in Him*, by His grace that is at work within us, and by the power of His Spirit.

Paul's Grief versus His Hope

The beautiful thing about the structure of Romans is that it goes from Paul's grief in Romans 7, where he confesses the reality of his brokenness, to his hope in Romans 8, where he declares the glory of God's grace.

In fact, Paul opens Romans 8 by boldly declaring:

> *There is no condemnation for those who belong to Christ Jesus.*
> (v. 1 NLT)

Notice Paul doesn't say "There remains only a little condemnation for those who belong to Christ Jesus." He's says, in no uncertain terms, "*no condemnation*"! None.

And he concludes Romans 8 with the absolute assurance of God's unwavering love in Christ:

And I am convinced that nothing can ever separate us from God's love. Neither death nor life, neither angels nor demons, neither our fears for today nor our worries about tomorrow—not even the powers of hell can separate us from God's love. No power in the sky above or in the earth below—indeed—nothing in all creation will ever be able to separate us from the love of God that is revealed in Christ Jesus our Lord.
(vv. 38–39 NLT)

Now, it appears that Paul is desperate to ensure that we don't miss the "nothing" part of this verse, so he takes the time to create a small but meaningful list of things that cannot separate us from God's love.

- death
- life
- angels
- demons
- fears for today
- worries about tomorrow
- the powers of hell
- power in the sky above or in the earth below

As worded in the Message, "Absolutely *nothing* can get between us and God's love because of the way that Jesus our Master has embraced us" (Romans 8:39 MSG).

God, who sees into the deep recesses of our heart, welcomes us at our very worst. And by His grace, He changes our identity from rebellious sinner to radically loved friend of God (Romans 9:25).

> God changes our identity from rebellious sinner to radically loved friend of God.

Nothing "But"

I am going to assume I am not the only one who reads a verse like Romans 8:38–39 and still thinks, *Surely, it's not that simple. Surely there is something we bring to the Cross that falls under the "everything but that" category.* And you know what we do? We put a *but* right in the middle of Paul's assurance.

We read, "Nothing *but* _____ can separate me from the love of God."

Now, maybe you put one big thing on that line. Or maybe you put several smaller things. Maybe you put both.

Can we get uncomfortable for a moment? Can we pause here and be honest with ourselves about those small and big things we have been holding on to—the things we fear have piled up and built a wall between us and God's love?

Maybe it's:

• your dark past
• your dark present

- your doubts
- your temper
- your prideful heart
- your anger
- your eating disorder
- your financial failure
- an abortion
- an affair
- a substance addiction
- a pornography addiction
- your divorce
- your dishonesty
- your lack of empathy or action for those suffering injustice
- your jealousy
- your imperfect parenting
- your lack of gratitude

Even as we read Paul's assurance, we hurry to fill in that blank with the painful "truths" about ourselves, with our short-comings, our sins, and our sorrows. In other words, with all the things we believe make us unworthy of the welcome and affection of God.

We fill in that blank with the "too dirty" things—the things that we believe are so deeply embedded into the fabric of our being that His blood cannot possibly reach, nonetheless wash clean, as white as snow (Isaiah 1:18).

We don't see ourselves through God's lens of mercy and grace. Instead, we see ourselves exactly as the enemy would have us see ourselves—through the lens of condemnation and shame.

God Is Not Mad at You

I'm not suggesting that our sin and rebellion don't break the heart of God. They absolutely do. But because of Jesus, our sin and rebellion don't make us less lovable to Him. The truth is that because of Jesus, God is not mad at us. How do we know? Because He's not mad at His Son. And when we are hidden in Christ, God loves us as He loves His Son (Romans 5:9–11).

> When we are hidden in Christ, God loves us as He loves His Son.

You are God's deeply loved daughter. You have been chosen and adopted as His child (Ephesians 1:4–5; Galatians 4:5). You are the delight of His life (Zephaniah 3:17). You are marked by His love. Not marked by your mistakes, not by your failures, not by the sins you've committed or the sins committed against you, but by His love.

You, dear one—the one who fears she has disappointed God and is damaging her kids—*you* bring your heavenly Father great joy.

Stumbling Toward Authentic Holiness

And here's the beautiful thing. As the truth of God's great grace penetrates and transforms our hearts, our desire to love God outweighs our desire to sin against Him. That's what grace does.

The grace of God makes our hearts break over the same things that break the heart of God. It melts the hardest hearts and inspires us, as new creations in Christ, to stumble toward authentic holiness through life in the Spirit (2 Corinthians 5:17).

So I need you to know this. Whatever it is that you insert on that "nothing but _____" line, His grace is big enough (Ephesians 1:6–8).

The Cross outweighs all of our offenses. The big ones. The little ones. And all the in-between ones. So we are free to get honest with ourselves about ourselves, and we are free to get honest with one another about whatever it is that makes us feel we are unworthy of God's affection and unwelcome at His table.

Jesus doesn't offer us a "nothing but _____" kind of love. His is an "even that" kind of love.

Standing in awe at the assurance of His absolute love and acceptance of us, a longing to love Him and follow Him is enlivened within our hearts. No longer fearful of God's rejection or disappointment—or dare I say it, disgust—we are set free to live as God's beloved. Trust me, I know. I think now's a good time to share a bit more of my story with you.

> Jesus doesn't offer us a "nothing but ___" kind of love. His is an "even that" kind of love.

CHAPTER 9

Our Struggle: I Can't Shed My Shame

God's Truth: Jesus Liberates Me from My Shame

It wasn't one of my finer moments. Signing the divorce papers, that is. Preachers' Kids don't do that. Preachers' Kids stay married forever. That's what I thought, at least. That's what I wanted more than anything. To get married only once.

And yet, even on my wedding day, as I stepped out of the horse-drawn carriage and onto the grassy green aisle that led to the water's edge, I feared I was not headed toward forever. There were too many red flags going into this marriage, too many warning bells going off in my head. But I chose to ignore them—all of them. I drowned out the doubts and alarms with the sound of wedding bells. The heart wants what it wants.

And yes, I know and believe that "all things are possible with God." I was offered that Scripture passage in Mark 10:27 more than once by well-intentioned people who told me to try harder, pray more, hope for the best, and keep hanging in there. All well-intentioned advice but hardly the thing I needed to hear in the awful and escalating situation I was in. Their advice just added to the crushing shame I already felt.

We spent the entirety of our eleven-month marriage in weekly Christian counseling—beginning the week after our "honeymoon." We had a good counselor. He saw us together; he saw us individually. I swear his heart actually hurt for us. But in the end I was forced to admit what I knew all along: this marriage was over before it started.

So, with eyes swollen shut from the countless tears shed, I walked into an attorney's office and whispered the words I never dreamed would be part of my story. "I'm here to file for divorce." And I walked out of that office certain I had forever lost God's pleasure and others' respect. Before that time, I hadn't known that a broken heart can physically hurt.

I entered the most painful and shameful season of my life.

The Merciless Shamer

I wasn't just broken. I was shattered. Shattered into so many pieces that I thought I could never be put back together again.

Unwanted. Unloved. Rejected. Shamed.

Despite God's assurances that *nothing* can separate us from His love, I was sure that my divorce was outside that assurance. Oh, trust me: I'd made plenty of other mistakes, done other un-holy things, and made many bad decisions before my divorce—

and I feared that these had already lessened God's love for me. But the divorce—that was the final blow, the one that actually separated me from His love, or so I believed.

The voice of the merciless shamer in my head was loud. *You are damaged goods. You are unworthy of God's love and favor. You are a failure. Your messy and broken life is of no value to Him. How can you call yourself a follower of Jesus and walk away from a marriage? And now you will have to work extra hard to regain God's pleasure and everyone else's respect.*

The voice of the merciless shamer in my head was loud: "You are damaged goods."

Those were the lies that played over and over in my head in the weeks and months that I walked—or, truthfully—crawled, through that divorce. I saw the bony finger of regret wagging in my face, and I heard shame's cackling voice, "Shame, shame, *shame on you!!*"

But it didn't take long for me to do what I've always done. I found the strength to pull myself up and get back to running on the achieve-aholic treadmill, determined to prove that I was still, somehow, some way, lovable.

When I got married, I'd moved from Atlanta, Georgia, to Charlotte, North Carolina, so it only made sense to return to Atlanta when things fell apart. I moved into my sister's basement and was given my old job back while I figured things out and got into my previous rhythm of life.

From the outside, it may have looked like things were coming together, but on the inside, I felt like I was dying. The sadness and the shame were too heavy to bear.

I wanted to hold on to Jesus in those dark and desperate days. But I didn't. I didn't have the strength to hold on to anything or anyone. However, Jesus *was* holding on to me. And He did not let me go. When I was faithless, He remained faithful (2 Timothy 2:13). When I lacked the strength to reach up, Jesus reached down. Right into my sin and pain, and He loved me at my very worst. He loved me at my darkest.

> When I lacked the strength to reach up, Jesus reached down. Right into my sin and brokenness, and He loved me at my very worst.

God's Grace-Filled Pursuit

While I was self-destructing and punishing myself for my sins, God was pursuing me with arms wide open. He longed to embrace me, pull me close, and whisper, "Jeannie, when I look at you, I don't see your failures. I see the perfection and righteousness of my Son, Jesus, covering you. And my love for you and my acceptance of you is wider and longer and deeper and higher than you can imagine. And I am going to continue doing what I have always done—I am going to keep on loving you" (Ephesians 3:17–19).

See, unbeknownst to me, God was using the dark days of my divorce to reveal the breadth of His grace to me. However, it took me years, almost ten to be exact, to see it—to see the grace that carried me through that incredibly painful and sometimes debilitating season in life.

That's the beautiful thing about grace. Even when we don't see it, it's there, working its way into every broken area of our lives. Healing and restoring. We don't have to be aware of grace for it to wield its healing and restoring power. God's undeserved love and favor is not limited by our awareness.

Over time, Jesus healed my broken heart, and He gave me the extraordinary gift of the love of my husband, Mike. This man of mine is everything I dreamed of but never thought I deserved. But you should know that when God brought us together, we were both pretty messy. Who am I kidding? We're both pretty messy now. We can barely believe God has entrusted four extraordinary boys to us. So hear me when I say we don't have this marriage thing tied up in a pretty bow. Marriage, like parenting, is sanctifying. But we love each other madly, and we work at making it work.

> Marriage, like parenting, is sanctifying.

But here's the thing. When I entered my marriage with Mike, I had deep wounds that were still healing and shame that still needed to be shed. I became pregnant soon after our wedding, and we went on to have three boys in five years. And because my sense of weakness and sinfulness only increased during those exhausting and overwhelming days of early motherhood—when I wasn't the perfect mom I was trying so hard to be—my sense of shame increased, too. Shame so powerful that I was crushed underneath it and couldn't escape it.

The Most Primitive Human Emotion

Dr. Brené Brown, renowned shame and vulnerability researcher, defines shame as the "intensely painful feeling or experience of believing that we are flawed and therefore unworthy of love and belonging."[1] In a recent interview she explained: "Shame is deadly. And I think we are swimming in it deep. Here's the bottom line with shame. The less you talk about it, the more you got it. . . . It's the most primitive human emotion we all feel—and the one no one wants to talk about."[2]

So, my fellow mom, we are going to talk about it! Because shame is robbing us from living in the freedom and the fullness of life that Jesus Christ secured for us!

Simply, shame is the lie that says *because I do unlovable things, I am an unlovable person.* When you make a mistake, shame says, "*You* are a mistake." It links what you do or what is done to you with the very essence of who you are. Shame is very real and very painful, and not one of us is immune to it.

> When you make a mistake, shame says, "*You* are a mistake."

In fact, pastor and author Scott Sauls writes this about shame:

Ever since Eden, every man, woman, and child has been facing a hidden battle with shame. The vague sense that there is something deeply wrong with us compels us to hide, blame, and run for cover. Left to ourselves, we are restlessly turned inward and desperately committed to some kind of self-salvation strategy. We work hard to create a counter-narrative to the shaming voice within and without.

What if there was a way for the cycle of shame to be broken in our lives? . . . My greatest joy as a Christian pastor is that I get to tell people that such a remedy exists. When Jesus allowed Himself to be stripped naked, spit upon, taunted, rejected, and made nothing on the cross—when He, the one who had nothing to be ashamed of, surrendered to the ruthless, relentless shaming that led to our redemption and healing—He accomplished our liberation from shame.[3]

Do you see that last sentence? When I first discovered Sauls' writing on shame, I read it several times over and let the truth of it settle into my soul. Jesus, king of world and lover of my soul, chose "ruthless, relentless shaming" to redeem and heal me. Even writing those words out now evokes so much emotion in me. I'll never get over it. After bearing the weight of my shame for so long, it slays me to think that the only reason I walk in freedom now is because Jesus willingly took my shame upon himself.

Friend, there *is* a remedy to the shame we feel! It's a person, and His name is Jesus. What a powerful name it is.

When Shame Spills over into Parenting

Now, I realize that for some of you, shame may be only a casual acquaintance, while for others, shame may be a best (bad) friend. Wherever you are on that spectrum, one thing's for sure: We have all experienced the crushing power of shame in some form or fashion. And if we've allowed that shame to hang out in our hearts, it's likely we've parented with shame.

Because what we live in is what we live out.

I hear from moms all the time who are living in shame over their inability to be a "good enough" mom for their kids. But that's only the beginning of their story. They are also devastated by how the shame they are living in spills over into their parenting. And then they feel even more ashamed. It's a vicious cycle that leaves moms terrified and hopeless.

Yes, sometimes we rely on shame to cajole our kids into certain behavior. Sometimes we project shame onto our kids because they aren't living up to our unrealistic expectations. But often, our shaming is the unintentional *living out* of our own shame. As one mom recently wrote to me through my blog,

> Thank you for writing so honestly about your parenting fails and God's forgiveness. It makes me feel not so alone in my own failure. My daughter had incredibly bad behavior this week. I get so angry and find it hard to forgive her for how she acts. Then I find it hard to forgive myself for my reaction to her. This parenting thing makes me feel so much shame, but I don't know what else to do.

As her email highlights, we all have a merciless critic in our heads that speaks condemnation to our hearts. That's the bad news. But here's the Good News. We also have a merciful Savior who hung on a cross, bearing the weight of our shame, so that we can walk in freedom.

We all have a merciless critic in our heads that speaks condemnation to our hearts. But! We also have a merciful Savior who bore our shame, so we can walk in freedom.

The Big Difference Between Condemnation and Conviction

When we sin and fall short of the glory of God, we need to know the vast difference between the voice of condemnation and the voice of conviction.

Condemnation comes from the enemy. It is the voice of shame urging us to believe that our heavenly Father is shaking His head at us in disappointment and disgust, His arms crossed and His heart closed.

> There's a vast difference between the voice of condemnation and the voice of conviction.

Conviction comes from the Holy Spirit. It is the voice of grace beckoning us to run to Jesus, repent, receive mercy, and run the race before us in His transforming power and grace (Romans 3:23–24).

Which voice are we going to listen to? The enemy uses shame to "steal and kill and destroy." But Jesus came to free us from shame so we can have "real and eternal life, more and better life than we ever dreamed of" (John 10:10 MSG).

The solution to our shame is never found in our own efforts or striving, but in Christ's perfect and substitutionary work. It comes only from being hidden in Him, resting in Him, and receiving His mercy and grace.

It's only when we stop thinking about ourselves and what we need to do, and start thinking about Jesus and what He did for us, that we can begin to break free from the shame. It's only when we stop asking how we can become the better version of ourselves and start saying, like Paul, "My only hope is Christ in me," that we will walk in freedom.

Our Identity in Christ

To put shame in its rightful place, we must receive the mercy and grace of God and enjoy the identity given to us by God in Jesus Christ. God's grace informs our identity. Here's who you *really* are in Christ:

You are *fully known*.

You are *fully accepted*.

You are *fully loved*.

That is who you are! And that is the essence of the Gospel—the Good News—that you and I need to be reminded of daily, perhaps hourly. We are not more loved and accepted in Jesus after we clean ourselves up, put on our Sunday best, and approach the throne of grace with a wholehearted commitment to do better tomorrow. No.

We are fully loved and accepted right now. Just as we are. Sinful and flawed. We were and are *secure* in God's love, all and only because of Jesus. When we fall into the pit, He doesn't throw us a ladder, He climbs into the pit and carries us out in His arms of grace. See, grace can't leave us where it finds us. It is the nature of grace to rescue us and

> When we fall into the pit, He doesn't throw us a ladder, He climbs into the pit and carries us out in His arms of grace.

progressively transform us into the image and likeness of Jesus (2 Corinthians 3:18).

This is not a pep talk. This is the *truth* of God's Word. These are not my words. These are His:

> *When we were utterly helpless, Christ came at just the*
> *right time and died for us sinners. Now, most people*
> *would not be willing to die for an upright person, though*
> *someone might perhaps be willing to die for a person who*
> *is especially good. But God showed his great love for us by*
> *sending Christ to die for us while we were still sinners.*
> (Romans 5:6–8 NLT)

Did you catch that? *While we were still sinners!* At our worst. At our darkest. Jesus gave His life for us!

Jesus absorbed every ounce of sin *and* shame for you and for me on the Cross. And if He didn't abandon us then, when He was absorbing the wrath of hell itself in our place, He isn't going to abandon us now. Jesus chose the nails with full knowledge of the ways we would break His heart with our rebellion.

He chose you then. He chooses you now. And you are never too lost to be found.

CHAPTER 10

Our Struggle: My Brokenness Makes Me Worthless

God's Truth: I Am God's Broken Beloved

My son Cal brought home a gift he'd made for me at school for Valentine's Day. For days, he'd been talking about how hard he'd been working on this gift, and I could tell how eager he was to give it to me.

But on the big day, he handed the wrapped present to me with hesitation and simply said, "I'm sorry, Mom," as he released it into my hands.

"Why are you sorry, baby?" I asked.

"You'll see," he replied with bowed head and downcast eyes.

I unwrapped the paper to discover a homemade, burnt-orange ceramic leaf. It was beautiful. And broken. And glued back together again. The repair job wasn't perfect, and cracks remained.

I looked at Cal, whose head was still bowed, and I lifted his chin, looked deep into his beautiful hazel eyes, and said, "Buddy, I love this leaf. I love it simply because your precious hands made it. It might be broken, but it's beautiful to me. I don't need it to be perfect. I love it just the way it is."

Cal's eyes lit up, and a big smile spread across his face. He put his head on my shoulder and said, "Thanks, Mom."

As we sat together, his head still on my shoulder, I said, "Now that I think of it, I am going to put this precious leaf on my desk as a reminder of how God feels about you and me. Buddy, we are imperfect and we carry brokenness, but Jesus loves us and welcomes us and *even wants us* just as we are . . ."

I felt him start to giggle as he lifted his head from my shoulder and responded, "I should have known you were going to say something like that." I gave him a tight squeeze, and whatever fear he'd been carrying about his offering not being "good enough" was lifted.

But here's the thing: I want you to know this isn't how I would have responded in my early days of parenting. Yes, I would have loved my son's leaf just as much, and I would have been quick to tell him so. But his broken leaf would not have reminded me about the way that God welcomes and loves us in our brokenness. I thought God wanted and welcomed only the "perfectly put together" version of me. It was *not* okay to not be okay. So just like my son feared bringing his broken pieces to me, I feared bringing my broken pieces to God.

> I thought God wanted and welcomed only the "perfectly put together" version of me. I feared bringing my broken pieces to God.

We Are Broken People

See, I thought my brokenness was something I could overcome if I just tried harder to fill in my cracks with good works. But if we turn to Scripture, we discover that because of the Fall, we actually enter this world sinful, fallen, broken people. There is no escaping the reality of our brokenness. We are broken people in broken relationships in a world that has been broken by sin. In fact, we aren't just broken. Scripture says we are *beyond* broken:

- We are dead in our sin (Ephesians 2:1; Romans 5:12).
- There is no one who does good, not even one (Psalm 14:3).
- Whoever keeps the whole law but fails in one point has become accountable for all of it (James 2:10).
- Scripture has shut up all men under sin (Galatians 3:22).
- Every intent of the thoughts of his heart was only evil continually (Genesis 6:5).
- The heart is fooled more than anything else, and is very sinful. Who can know how bad it is (Jeremiah 17:9).
- Surely, I was sinful at birth, sinful from the time my mother conceived me (Psalm 51:5).
- For all have sinned and fall short of the glory of God (Romans 3:23).
- And if we say we have no sin, we deceive ourselves and the truth is not in us (1 John 1:7–8).

That's pretty bad news. No sugarcoating there. And even worse: Brokenness is not just a temporary feeling we experience when we do something bad or when something bad is done to us. It's not just a "season" we walk through. It is actually the state in which we exist and live on this side of heaven.

But there's more to the story. See, the bad news is actually the doorway to the Good News. Because it is only when we finally accept how dead we are in sin and how far we've fallen short of God's holy requirements that we can begin to embrace and celebrate the necessity of God's grace.

> It is only when we finally accept how far we've fallen short of God's holy requirements that we can begin to embrace and celebrate the necessity of God's grace.

Brennan Manning framed this beautifully when he wrote: "To be alive is to be broken; to be broken is to stand in need of grace."[1]

So essentially, if we're breathing, we're broken. And if we're broken, we're in need of Christ.

As Manning goes on to write, "Jesus comes not for the super-spiritual but for the wobbly and the weak-kneed who know they don't have it all together, and who are not too proud to accept the handout of amazing grace."[2]

But this is where many of us get stuck. I know I did. We don't want to acknowledge or accept our brokenness. We don't want to admit that we don't have it all together—because we fear that would mean we are a disappointment to God. We much prefer to keep working our way toward wholeness. Or better said, perfection.

But, as demonstrated by what we recently read of Paul's

experience in Romans 7 and 8, the focus of the Christian life isn't overcoming our brokenness and getting better at being good. It was Paul's increasing awareness of just how broken he was in the flesh that made him so grateful for grace and reliant on the transforming work of the Holy Spirit. And the same is true for us. When we accept how utterly dependent we are on the grace of God and the transforming power of the Holy Spirit, we will stop fighting our brokenness and embrace our belovedness.

His Broken Beloved

The only way to grow in holiness is to accept that we are *both* broken sinners and beloved children of God. We are the broken beloved.

While we are already perfect in Christ, we are not yet whole in the flesh. Indeed, the wholeness we *crave* is coming! Because Jesus was broken for us, we will, for all eternity, be whole. But until then, we have the peace and the power and the presence of God to carry us through this broken world as we await the assurance of our wholeness in the life to come. Until then . . . we are His broken beloved.

> By God's grace, we are not *just* broken. We are the broken beloved.

We see this truth revealed in God's Word:

> *Dear friends, we are God's children now. But it has not yet been shown to us what we are going to be.*

We know that when He comes again, we will be
like Him because we will see Him as He is.
(1 John 3:2 NLV)

For now, we see only a reflection as in a mirror; then
we shall see face to face. Now I know in part; then
I shall know fully, even as I am fully known.
(1 Corinthians 13:12)

While we wait for God's "until then," it helps to remember that my brokenness is the very thing that keeps me close to Jesus. Being aware of my brokenness allows me to experience the goodness, the faithfulness, the kindness, and the undying love of Jesus. Let's not miss the profound beauty and blessing that can be experienced in this place of broken belovedness.

So I want to encourage you, dear mom. If you don't feel whole, or if you don't feel like God has glued all your pieces back together so that no cracks remain, don't lose hope. It doesn't mean God's not at work in your life. Because you are His child, He is indeed at work, wooing you to Himself and crafting you in His likeness. And He will make good on His promise of wholeness when sin is wiped out for good. In the meantime, His love and light inside you can shine through your cracks, to the glory of His grace.

It's Okay to Admit You're Not Okay

So, what shall we do with our brokenness until Jesus returns? We bring our brokenness to God. God's specialty is rescuing and redeeming broken people and carrying out His purpose through them. In fact, it's only when we acknowledge and accept our own brokenness that we will finally be free to live the authentic and abundant

> God's specialty is rescuing and redeeming broken people and carrying out His purpose through them.

lives Jesus secured for us, and be empowered to lead our kids in doing the same.

The breathtakingly beautiful truth about grace is that *it's okay to not be okay*. And it's okay to *admit* you're not okay. We can be honest about it because we have a Savior who was more than okay. He was perfect. And He has us covered (Romans 3:22). Oh, sweet freedom!

So grace frees us to be honest about our brokenness with ourselves. And grace frees us to be honest about our brokenness with God. But there's still more! Grace also frees us to be honest about our brokenness with our kids *and* with one another.

Grace Frees Us to Live Transparently

We will soon devote our attention to how grace frees us to be honest with our kids about our brokenness, but here, I want to focus on how grace frees us to be honest with one another. And to do so, I want to begin by borrowing a question asked by Elyse

Fitzpatrick in her brilliant book, *Good News for Weary Women.*
She writes:

> If it is true that we are all sinners in need of grace, and if,
> most happily, Jesus loves sinners, then why don't we all stop
> pretending to be something other than what we are?

It's a really good question, right? If we are all broken, and if
Jesus loves the broken, why are we so afraid to share our brokenness with each other?

In light of this question, Elyse encourages us to:

> Live our life transparently so others will see that Jesus loves
> the weak, the weary, the wounded, and the sinner, and per-
> haps they, too, will be emboldened to stop faking it. . . . We
> have been called to help others give up their masks and walk
> into transparency, vulnerability, and authenticity. . . . Take a
> good long look at yourself and laugh at God's sense of hu-
> mor in calling you a saint. And while you're at it, admit the
> truth about yourself to someone else—that person knows it
> anyway. And then you two can chuckle together and rejoice
> in grace.[3]

Living transparently—as God's broken beloved—is conta-
gious. When we are honest about our brokenness, those around
us will be inspired to do the same. They will be freed to be honest
about how fragile they feel. That is how we use our brokenness
to bless others.

And honestly, with whom would you rather enjoy a cup of
coffee? The woman who wants to impress you or the woman

who wants to bless you? As we remember who we are in Christ, we can live transparently, blessing rather than impressing one another. And together we can be impressed by the perfection of Christ and the righteousness He has bestowed on us both. Doesn't that sound so good?

> As we remember who we are in Christ, we can live transparently, blessing rather than impressing one another.

I'm not discounting that we are real women, fighting real sin, carrying real burdens, and experiencing real pain. I feel the weight of my brokenness daily. But just beyond the bad news that we are far worse off than we want to admit is the good news that Jesus loves and welcomes the broken.

The Way of Compassion and Comfort

Think about this: *Why are moms so hard on each other?* Could it be because we're so hard on ourselves? The supermom myth has done quite a job on us. We try to live up to impossible standards, and we hold others to those standards as well. However, when we are honest about our own imperfection and brokenness, we become more compassionate toward the imperfection and brokenness of others.

Listen, I know we know this, but I think we need to be reminded of it all the time: *There is no VIP section at the foot of the Cross.* Every single one of us comes to the Cross with nothing to offer but our need. The mom who takes cupcakes to every school party needs Jesus just as much as the mom so strung out on cocaine that she can't take care of her kids at all. In this world, we are constantly stacked against one another, but at the Cross, we stand alongside one another, each desperately in need of grace, which is freely given in Christ.

In this knowledge we are free to serve and love and be "the least of these" (Matthew 25:45), because we are secure in being—first and foremost—God's beloved, treasured daughters. Knowing we are God's broken beloved frees us to bless, not impress, one another and to have grace-filled hearts as we take the hand of the also-broken-beloved mom beside us.

When we remember our brokenness in light of our belovedness, we will naturally find ourselves trading in our old ways of comparing and competing for the ways of the Father—the ways of compassion and comfort (2 Corinthians 1:3–5). Who doesn't want to live like that? Of course, we all do!

But—we also can't help but question, "Hold up. This sounds wonderful, but what about all the Bible verses that tell us we should pursue holiness and 'walk in a manner worthy of the calling to which you have been called' (Ephesians 4:1). Are we just supposed to accept that we are broken people, not pursue godliness, and not encourage one another to do the same?"

I'm so glad you asked. Let's go there now.

CHAPTER 11

Our Struggle: I Must Live Up to the Gospel

God's Truth: I Am Called to Live Out of the Gospel

I have a close friend who often jokes, "It must be hard living in your head." She's not a (recovering) type A perfectionist like I am, and she can't fathom life inside my type A brain.

But what I've discovered in talking with moms who wouldn't necessarily label themselves as "type A perfectionists" is that we all can have some pretty unrealistic expectations of ourselves.

A Facebook post by a friend framed this well. She writes:

I never thought I'd be a perfect mother, and yet it always seems to surprise me when I'm not. Maybe you are like me, someone who never really tries to be perfect but gets sidelined each time you fall short of some unspoken standard. Or maybe you absolutely try to achieve perfection but feel like a failure each time you miss the mark. I imagine every single mother falls into one of these categories. As moms, either we aim for perfection and feel shame when we miss, or we simply hope for the best and crumble when reality leaves us defeated. Then what?

I think we can all relate to her quandary. Perfectionist or not, we frequently feel like failures when we don't measure up. No doubt, some of the pressure we feel comes from our culture's impossible standards. But, truth be told, a lot of the pressure Christian moms experience is rooted in what Scriptures says. Or better said, what we *think* Scripture says.

Sadly, one of the biggest obstacles to living in the fullness and freedom of God's love is misinterpreting Scripture. And there is no better example of this than how we tend to interpret what Jesus taught in the Sermon on the Mount in the Gospel of Matthew, chapters 5 through 7. So, I want us to spend some time with this text.

> Perfectionist or not, we frequently feel like failures when we don't measure up.

"Be Ye Perfect"

In this well-known sermon—the Sermon on the Mount—Jesus gives His authoritative interpretation of God's law and addresses almost every life topic imaginable: murder, anger, adultery, lust, divorce, loving our neighbor, giving to the needy, prayer and fasting, storing up treasures in heaven rather than on earth, worry, judging others, and much more.

As you know, I am a girl who spent most of her life thinking that the Bible was an instruction manual, so you can imagine what I did with the Sermon on the Mount. I basically boiled these three chapters down to a checklist of dos and don'ts.

But it's what Jesus says right in the middle of this sermon—in Matthew 5:48—that energized the overachiever in me and led me to conclude that, ultimately, the Christian life is about pursuing perfection.

Jesus said, *"Be perfect, therefore, as your heavenly Father is perfect"* (NIV).

That's pretty clear, right? Be perfect!

So that is precisely what I aimed to do. Of course, I failed daily and miserably, but perfection remained the goal because, well, I wanted to make Him proud of me.

And, as if that wasn't enough pressure, I also thought God's reputation was riding on my shoulders because of how I read and understood what Jesus said shortly before "be perfect" in verse 16: "Let your light shine before others, that they may see your good deeds and glorify your Father in heaven" (NIV).

Basically, I thought being a Christian was about being perfect to keep God proud and doing good deeds so others would see what perfect Christians do and would want to be one, too.

Many years ago, however, I was introduced to Gospel-centered teachers who reminded me of what I was taught in my childhood but had long forgotten—the Sermon on the Mount isn't a sermon on how to earn Brownie points with God and save souls in the process. It's a sermon that does two things simultaneously: First, it shows us the *standard* by which we should seek to live as His ambassadors in a world that is not yet fully transformed. And, second, it shows us our *inability* to live up to God's high standard of righteousness by our own power.

The Sermon on the Mount reveals our utter inability to "be ye perfect" *and* our desperate need for the One who was perfect on our behalf.

In other words, the Sermon on the Mount reveals our utter inability to "be ye perfect" *and* our desperate need for the One who was perfect on our behalf. So let's take a look at this passage with that in mind.

God Wants Our Hearts

It's important to note that as Jesus is teaching the crowd, He knows He also has the attention of the Pharisees. The Pharisees were the guys who were really good at being good. They worked hard at meeting God's demands for godliness, and they did a great job—on the outside. And they were very proud of their external "perfection."

To better explain the Pharisees, let me interject with a short story about my own unclean heart.

There was a woman who had been intentionally unkind to me and handled a situation between us cruelly. Her words and actions hurt me deeply. She knew it and I knew it, but she had no intention of confessing it and/or repairing the situation.

Several months after this incident, we ended up running into each other at an event. When I saw her across the room, I knew I had two options: I could either pretend I didn't see her and attempt to avoid her, or I could "kill her with kindness," as the expression goes. Well, I went with the latter.

I approached her with a smile, gave her a hug, exchanged quick pleasantries, and then excused myself.

That evening I told my husband about running into this woman and how I handled the situation. To which he responded, "Wow, babe. That's really great. I know she really hurt you, and I'm so glad you were able to be kind to her and forgive her even though she never apologized."

But before my husband could finish his sentence, the Holy Spirit got all up in my business, and conviction hit me to the core.

"Actually, babe," I confessed, "there is nothing to be proud of here. I didn't approach her with real love in my heart. My true intention was not pure. Was it good that I was kind? I guess. But I was only trying to make a point to her."

In other words, doing the right thing with the wrong heart motive still misses the mark. Ouch.

What Jesus is demonstrating in the Sermon on the Mount is that God actually cares about what's on the inside—in our hearts. God requires *more* than good external behavior. His high standard is a pure and perfect *heart*. A heart that loves Him above *all* else. Meaning, doing the right thing with the wrong motive still fails to meet the moral standard called for in the Sermon on the Mount. So even if

> God's high standard is a pure and perfect *heart*. A heart that loves Him above *all* else.

we think we are getting it all right in our outward actions, we aren't getting it all right in our hearts—at least not to the extent that God's law demands.

The Pharisees didn't even get close to pure hearts. Neither do we. But once again, what seems like bad news is actually the doorway to the Good News! The complete righteousness that

God requires was satisfied by Jesus. Jesus was pure and perfect in His heart, on our behalf. And because of Him—and only because of Him—we are declared righteous before God!

In the Sermon on the Mount, Jesus reveals our brokenness and desperation *so that* we will *finally be set free* from trying to achieve an unachievable righteousness and *so that* we will *fall in awe and wonder* at the feet of the One who achieved it for us. One of the primary functions of the Law is to demonstrate the impossibility of keeping it, and thus it leads us to Jesus for our righteousness. As we read in Romans 5:20:

> *God's law was given so that all people could see how sinful they were. But as people sinned more and more, God's wonderful grace became more abundant. So just as sin ruled over all people and brought them to death, now God's wonderful grace rules instead, giving us right standing with God and resulting in eternal life through Jesus Christ our Lord.*
> (NLT)

Indeed, "it's God's gift of the law that drives us to the Savior who fulfilled the law in our place."[1]

The Crucial Distinction between the Law and the Gospel

Stick with me here because this distinction is essential to our ability to walk in freedom. Rightly distinguishing between Law and Gospel is "the most difficult and the highest art of Christians."[2]

Both the Law and the Gospel are indispensable in the Christian life and the pursuit of holiness.

The Law tells us what to do. It is holy, righteous, and good (Romans 7:12); it is perfect, trustworthy, and more precious than gold (Psalm 19:7–10). And, as the psalmist writes, "Blessed is the one . . . whose delight is in the law of the Lord and who meditates on his law day and night. That person is like a tree planted by streams of water, which yields its fruit in season and whose leaf does not wither—whatever they do prospers" (Psalm 1:1–3).

The Gospel tells us what's already been done in Jesus Christ. "For everyone has sinned; we all fall short of God's glorious standard. Yet God, with undeserved kindness, declares that we are righteous. He did this through Christ Jesus when he freed us from the penalty for our sins" (Romans 3:23–24 NLT). That's why the gospel is called the Good News.

C. F. W. Walther explains: "Law is anything that refers to what we are to do," while "the Gospel, or the Creed, is any doctrine or word of God that does not require works from us and does not command us to do something but bids us simply to accept as a gift the gracious forgiveness of sins and the everlasting bliss offered us."[3]

I've heard this important distinction expressed more simply, like this: The Law says *do*. The Gospel says *done*. And reading God's Word through *that* lens changes everything.

> The Law says *do*. The Gospel says *done*.

Do you see how very good the Good News of the Gospel is for those of us who don't feel good enough? We no longer need to pretend that we can perfectly pull it off. In God's eyes, because of Jesus, we are already "perfect," just as our heavenly Father is perfect (Matthew 5:48).

Gratitude Inspires Obedience, and Obedience Reaps Blessing

Let's not confuse being grateful for God's grace with making light of our sin. In fact, it is our *gratitude* for God's unrelenting love that inspires *obedience*.

See, our sin can and does have devastating consequences on our lives and on the lives of our children. My sin is what nailed my Savior to the cross. My sin gives birth to death (James 1:15). There is nothing about that to be celebrated. What *is* worthy of celebration is that my sinless Savior paid for my sin-stained life on the Cross, securing my acceptance before God.

> My sinless Savior paid for my sin-stained life on the Cross, securing my acceptance before God.

What we must realize is that increasing the pressure (just try harder, just do more) does not lead us away from sin. Instead, it often leads us deeper into sin, as we rely more and more on our own power; and it leads us deeper into despair, as we realize we don't have what it takes.

What does lead us away from sin is awe of the One who became sin for us so that we might become the righteousness of God. Gratitude for Christ's obedience on our behalf inspires our obedience to God. And here's the other thing: Obedience reaps blessing. Blessing doesn't come with sin. It comes with obedience. As James writes:

> But whoever looks intently into the perfect law that gives freedom, and continues in it—not forgetting what they have heard, but doing it—they will be blessed in what they do.
> (James 1:25 NIV)

Genuine obedience to the "perfect law"—through dependence on the Holy Spirit—brings freedom and blessing.

And still! Obedience is not what makes us "right with God." It's Jesus and only Jesus, as we see in God's Word below:

> For no one can ever be made right with God by doing what the law commands. The law simply shows us how sinful we are. But now God has shown us a way to be made right with him without keeping the requirements of the law, as was promised in the writings of Moses and the prophets long ago. We are made right with God by placing our faith in Jesus Christ. And this is true for everyone who believes, no matter who we are.
> (Romans 3:20–22 NLT)

Knowing this—that it is only because of Jesus that we are set free from the pressure to get it all right—creates a new dynamic for obedience! The Good News is not only freeing, it's transformative! Knowing the lengths to which Jesus went to rescue us opens us up to the Holy Spirit's transforming work in our lives.

The grace of God inspires obedience that stems from desire, not duty. Gratitude, not guilt. Awe, not obligation (Romans 6:14; Titus 2:11–12). And as Paul helps us understand, *this* is precisely the kind of obedience that God wants.

> The grace of God inspires obedience that stems from desire, not duty. Gratitude, not guilt. Awe, not obligation.

Living Out of the Gospel, Not Up to It

What I love about the apostle Paul is that he is just as clear in his charge to *pursue holiness* as he is in his *confession of unholiness*. He assures us that we are still responsible for living a holy life. As we see in Ephesians 4:1, where Paul clearly exhorts us: "Lead a life worthy of your calling."

The old Jeannie would have read that verse and again thought, *Marching orders! Live a life worthy of Jesus' love and affection, lest you lose it by letting Him down.* Which is why I'm so thankful for the wisdom Paul Tripp sheds on Ephesians 4. His words have been incredibly helpful to me in making sense of the tension I've experienced between my desire to *pursue holy living* while also *resting in the perfection of Christ.*

Unfortunately, I think we have misunderstood and mishandled this passage. The common theme is, "It's your job to live up to the standard of the Gospel." Once I heard someone basically preach, "Get your act together. If you don't, you'll bring shame to the name of Jesus."

If that's the message of this verse, we're in trouble. You and I have no ability to walk in a manner worthy of the

Gospel. If you think you do, you've underestimated the power of indwelling sin.

Don't get me wrong—I firmly believe that the Bible calls us out of sin and into a radically transformed lifestyle of righteousness. We're no longer free to do as our sinful hearts desire. We've been bought with a price and are called to glorify God with our actions (1 Corinthians 6:20).

That being said, the flow of Ephesians is not to "live up to" the Gospel, but rather "live out of" the Gospel. It's an incredibly important distinction.

Instead of saying "Here's the standard . . . now live up to it," the apostle Paul encourages the believer to "live out of" the Gospel through the power of the indwelling Holy Spirit.[4]

There's a radical difference between "up to" and "out of."

We see a similar flow again in Ephesians 5:1, where Paul continues his charge to pursue authentic holiness. He writes, "Imitate God, therefore, in everything you do, because you are his dear children."

Did you notice the word *because*? Paul isn't telling us to imitate God to *become* His dear children. He is charging us to live out of the assurance that we *already* are. Imitate God *because* you already are His child. Not to gain status or favor. But because you already have it.

> Paul isn't telling us to imitate God to *become* His dear children. He is charging us to live out of the assurance that we *already* are.

Imperatives and Indicatives

I'm baffled by how I managed to live most of my life reading the Bible basically cover to cover without ever understanding this distinction, which the *ESV Gospel Transformation Bible* explains so clearly: "The imperatives of the Christian life—what we are called to do as we follow Christ by faith—are founded on and flow from the indicative of the Christian life—who we are in Christ by faith. Moreover, every imperative in the Christian life is provided to us as a gracious admonition from God so that we might glorify Him and enjoy Him as we live the free and abundant life we have in Christ—who is the way, the truth, and the life."[5]

This distinction changed everything about how I read the Bible and, therefore, everything about how I lived and how I parented.

When we remember how Jesus perfectly obeyed the Father on our behalf, we realize that the Christian life isn't being "perfect" or even "good enough." Jesus was and is perfect, just as His Father in heaven is perfect. And obedience becomes a thing of beauty, not burden. What a tremendous relief!

CHAPTER 12

Our Struggle: I Must Work Hard to Please God

God's Truth: I Am Set Free for Freedom

The boys left the door wide open as they ran in and out of the house between the kitchen and the backyard (their two favorite places) on a lazy summer evening. To no one's surprise, several pesky flies made their way into our home. When we sat down for dinner around the kitchen counter, one particularly annoying fly decided to join us and relentlessly pursue our food as we attempted to eat. Finally, I set my fork down and got up, determined to catch it so we could eat in peace.

This fly was a fast one, and my boys cheered me on while I chased it in circles. But it refused to surrender. Finally, I thought, *Maybe, if I talk to him and tell him what I'm trying to do, he'll surrender.* (Desperate times call for desperate measures!) "Come on, little guy, I am trying to catch you to set you free." Don't judge me, but I may have even quoted Scripture. The one we'd memorized the week before was in the forefront of my mind and seemed fitting. "My plans for you are good. My plans for you are not to harm you but to give you a future." (A slight knockoff of Jeremiah 29:11.)

As you might suspect, Scripture didn't inspire the fly. He didn't surrender, but he did eventually run out of steam. (I'm nothing if not determined.) When the fly rested on a windowsill, it was my opportunity to gently cup my hands around him, carry him outside, and set him free. I didn't want to capture him to hurt him. I captured him to set him free. To give him life. To give him freedom.

> Jesus relentlessly pursues us to set us free.

It's a bit like what Jesus does with us. He relentlessly pursues us to set us free, to live in freedom (Galatians 5:1).

What Is Freedom—Really?

The enemy wants us to believe that Jesus pursues us to do anything *but* set us free. In fact, he's done a good job of convincing people that the Christian life is primarily about being stuck in a joyless system of religious rules and regulations. So I think it would be helpful for us to clarify what this complex word—*freedom*—means in the Christian life.

Our culture tells us that freedom is the ability to do what we want and to live as we please. But if we've spent any time seeking this kind of freedom, we know it's a phony freedom full of empty promises. And phony freedom always leads to disappointment and ultimate destruction.

The freedom that Christ offers is radically different. It's a freedom that looks much like the kind illustrated in the following story. Perhaps you know it?

There is an old story about a man who attended a slave auction to bid on a slave girl. As the girl looked at the man bidding on her, she figured he was just another rich man who would buy her, then abuse her.

The man won the bid, and as he was walking away with his property, he said, "Young lady, you are free."

She said, "What does that mean?"

"It means you are free."

"Does that mean," she said, "that I can say whatever I want to say?"

The man said, "Yes, my dear, you can say whatever you want to say."

"Does that mean," she said, "that I can be whatever I want to be?"

He said, "Yes, you can be whatever you want to be."

"Does that mean that I can go wherever I want to go?"

He said, "Yes, you can go wherever you want to go."

The girl, with tears streaming down her face, said, "Then I will go with you."[1]

This man went down to the slave block and set a young girl free. Jesus Christ came down to earth to set you and me free. And the freedom Christ purchased for us, not with money but with his very life, is what inspires us to say, like the slave girl, "Then I will go with you." Jesus freed *you and me* from slavery and when we truly grasp the magnitude of this, we will desire to stay close to Him. To do life like Him. To love others like Him.

Set Free from What?

Now I realize that most of us don't tend to think of ourselves as enslaved, right? In fact, I bet most of us would say we live "free lives." Let's turn to Paul's writing in Galatians 5 to work this out. Paul writes:

> *It is for freedom that Christ has set us free. Stand firm, then, and do not let yourselves be burdened again by a yoke of slavery.*
> (Galatians 5:1 NIV)

These two sentences hold extraordinarily Good News for us. Paul says, *"It is for freedom that Christ has set us free."* We've been set free for what? For freedom! *"Great! But freedom from what?"* From the "yoke of slavery."

The yoke of slavery is the burden we feel to gain God's favor through perfect obedience to the law. We are all desperate for God's favor, but the demands of the law are just too rigorous. Indeed, the weight of those demands is *intolerable* because there's no way we can accomplish it! Paul is saying, "Don't let yourselves be burdened again by striving for perfection to keep God pleased. Don't go back to that old way of life because no one can handle that pressure. No one can be pure and perfect in their actions *and* in their heart."

No one, that is, but Jesus. He's the only One, my friend. Not me, not you. Jesus is the only One.

Though faced with the same temptations we face and pursued by Satan to the same sinfulness, Jesus remained without blemish or blame. The sinless, spotless, Lamb of God. He was the only One who can (and did!) fulfill the rigorous demands of the law, securing

God's eternal favor for us (1 Peter 1:18–19). This can mean only one thing: it's the Cross of Christ, not our progress or performance, that makes us pleasing to God.

> It's the Cross of Christ, not our progress or performance, that makes us pleasing to God.

But living in light of that truth can be *so* hard, right?

I think Martin Luther was on to something when he said, "To be convinced in our hearts that we have forgiveness of sins and peace with God by grace alone is the hardest thing."[2] The hardest thing, indeed. Which is precisely why even Christians who have been "set free" struggle to live in freedom.

Three Paths to Love and Acceptance

In our quest for freedom, we can go about life in one of three ways.

1. We can live *for* God's love and acceptance.
2. We can try to ignore God's love and acceptance.
3. We can live *from* God's love and acceptance.

Let's talk about each of these.

Living *for* God's Love and Acceptance

When we live *for* God's love and acceptance, we try to earn and keep His pleasure in us by our best-ness, by our obedience, by our effort to "get better and try harder" to live a more "Christiany" life.

If you've tried this approach, as I have, and you are willing to be honest, you'll admit that no matter how hard you try, it is utterly impossible to run at that pace for very long. Along the road, we keep bumping into our brokenness, stumbling over our sin, and feeling weighed down by our weaknesses. And at some point, we all collapse from the physical exhaustion and the soul dehydration.

The apostle Paul writes about how he tried this approach, too:

We know very well that we are not set right with God by rule-keeping but only through personal faith in Jesus Christ. How do we know? We tried it—and we had the best system of rules the world has ever seen! Convinced that no human being can please God by self-improvement, we believed in Jesus as the Messiah so that we might be set right before God by trusting in the Messiah, not by trying to be good.
(Galatians 2:16 MSG)

Being set right before God, Paul says, doesn't result from following the best system of rules and "trying to be good." And no plan for self-improvement will cut it. Faith in Jesus is the only way. We can't supplement His perfect work.

> Being set right before God doesn't happen from "trying to be good." We can't supplement the perfect work of Christ.

Maybe you've tried to supplement Christ's perfect work like I have. Maybe you put your feet on the floor in the morning and say something like, "Lord, today I will try harder to _____. I will do *this* and I will do *that*. Do you see me, Lord? I'm trying!" But the story always ends in despair, because no matter how hard we try, we can't be pure and perfect in our actions and in our hearts, as we discovered in the last chapter.

This doesn't mean that we shouldn't heed what we read in verses like Hebrews 12:14 that say, "Work at living in peace with everyone, and work at living a holy life." We absolutely should work at obeying God's commands and living a Christian life. But our motivation to pursue godliness and do good works is to be grounded in the grace God has shown us in Christ, not in an effort to produce grace in our lives, and it certainly can't be accomplished in our own strength.

And here's the thing. Living for God's love and approval typically leads us straight to the second way we can approach life—ignoring God's love and approval and living for our own—because the intolerable burden of keeping God happy is just too much.

Ignoring God's Love and Acceptance

This approach to life entails ignoring or simply rejecting our soul-deep, God-designed, longing for His love and approval and settling for our own. As Elyse Fitzpatrick writes:

> Our principal concern is not that we don't have God's approval; it's that we don't really care that we do. Need proof? Have you ever thought, I know that God forgives me but I just can't forgive myself? Aside from the fact that self-forgiveness isn't even hinted at in Scripture, this impulse to seek okay-ness in our own eyes is a clear indication of our apathy about God's opinion and our bondage to our own.
>
> For Christians, though, it should be a different story. And it is—at least in part. I think most Christians sincerely

do want to please God, and yet somehow we have failed to make the connection between the work of Jesus Christ and our own work. . . . Most of us know that our sins have been forgiven because of Jesus' death on Calvary, but we've never thought deeply about what His sinless life and bodily resurrection might mean when we're faced with our failures.[3]

I believe this struggle stems primarily from our culture's insistence that we just need to do a better job "loving ourselves" because we're really not *that* bad. We try to minimize the magnitude of our sins and shortcomings so we can feel better about how we're doing. What we don't realize is that even this way of living is a form of slavery—we are enslaved to our ever-fluctuating opinion of ourselves. On our good days, we think we're awesome. On our bad days, we think we're awful. What we *really* need is to be rescued from ourselves!

This is not to suggest that we should see ourselves as "worthless." God is clear—you are of great worth in his eyes: "And the very hairs on your head are all numbered. So don't be afraid; you are more valuable to God than a whole flock of sparrows" (Luke 12:7 NLT).

When we find ourselves overly concerned with what we think of ourselves, that's a signal that we don't have our eyes squarely on the face of Jesus.

But nowhere in Scripture do we find God telling us to do a better job of "loving ourselves." Rather, we read: "And so we know and rely on the love God has for us" (1 John 4:16 NIV). Can we read that verse again? We are to "know and rely" on God's love for us. Not our love for ourselves. His is the only steadfast and trustworthy love. When we find ourselves overly concerned with what *we* think of ourselves, that's a signal that we don't have our eyes squarely on the face of Jesus.

Slavery to "self-approval" is understandable for anyone who has not put her hope in Christ, but those of us who *have* should be walking in freedom. Sometimes, we just don't know how to get there. We've been living *for* God's love for so long that we can't fathom the freedom in simply living *from* it. It seems wrong. Too easy. And yet it's exactly what Christ came to do. The Gospel gives us permission to confess we are not "good enough" on our own and invites us to rest in *His* enough-ness. And when we do, our self-approval becomes irrelevant.

Which leads us right to the third way we can go about life.

Living *from* God's Love and Acceptance

Living *from* God's love is accompanied by untold blessings.

When we live *from* God's love and acceptance, we live in the assurance—the confidence—that God's eternal love and acceptance and favor and delight and approval is already entirely ours, all because of what Jesus Christ did for us through His perfect keeping of the law on our behalf. We trust there is absolutely nothing—not a single sin or weakness—that can make God stop loving us. Or liking us.

When we live *from* God's love, we can rest in the assurance that our worth is not determined by what we have or haven't done in the past or what we can or can't do now. It is firmly anchored in the far surpassing worth of Jesus Christ on our behalf (Titus 3:5).

Living *from* God's love leads to freedom from the "intolerable burden" of striving for what is already ours in Christ. We are free to live as God's beloved—fully known, fully accepted, and fully loved. You know, that thing we all crave.

When we live *from* God's love, we live free from slavery to self-reliance. We live free from proving we are worthy of love and belonging. We shed our shame and embrace our new identity in Christ.

When we live *from* God's love, we find that "our delight is in the law of the Lord, and on it we meditate day and night" (Psalm 1). We discover that God's Word is where joy and hope and wisdom are found. We spend time in God's Word because we *want* to, not because we *have* to. We do it because we love it. We do it because it's what takes us deeper and deeper into the heart of the One who loved us and gave His life for us.

> When we live *from* God's love, we discover the true rest our souls crave. The kind that keeps us fit for the journey.

When we live *from* God's love, we discover the true rest our souls crave. The kind that keeps us fit for the journey.

Now, maybe after hearing all this, you're wondering, "That sounds great but what does that look like on a practical level?" Well, the good news is, Paul lays it out simply, and the Message paraphrase brings his meaning home.

What actually took place is this: I tried keeping rules and working my head off to please God, and it didn't work. So I quit being a "law man" so that I could be God's man. Christ's life showed me how, and enabled me to do it. I identified myself completely with him. Indeed, I have been crucified with Christ. My ego is no longer central. It is no longer

important that I appear righteous before you or have your
good opinion, and I am no longer driven to impress God.
Christ lives in me. The life you see me living is not "mine,"
but it is lived by faith in the Son of God, who loved me and
gave himself for me. I am not going to go back on that.
Is it not clear to you that to go back to that old rule-keeping,
peer-pleasing religion would be an abandonment of everything
personal and free in my relationship with God? I refuse to do
that, to repudiate God's grace. If a living relationship with God
could come by rule-keeping, then Christ died unnecessarily.
(Galatians 2:19–21)

Let's break that down, because for those of us who are prone to ask for the checklist of things we can "do" to live freely, here is the part we've been waiting for.

Checklist
1. Quit trying to please God by keeping the rules.
2. Identify yourself completely with Christ.
3. Stop trying to impress God.
4. Live by faith in Christ's work on your behalf.
5. Refuse to reject God's grace.

I'll admit, Paul's list is not your typical checklist. It's not a "go forth and do" checklist. It's a "quit, stop, receive, accept, enjoy" kind of list. That's how it is with grace.

The *ESV Gospel Transformation Bible* frames it this way: "The gospel sabotages any notion of legalism or performance-based acceptability with God. The only thing we bring to Jesus is our need. All we offer is the admission that we have nothing to offer."[4]

It is only when we can sing with confidence, "Nothing in my hands I bring, simply to thy cross I cling" that we begin walking in freedom.

Believing we are saved (and sanctified!) by grace inspires us to repent and embrace new obedience. Saving faith is what produces good works—not the other way around. When we believe we are His beloved, we will live like His beloved.

> When we really believe we are His beloved, we will live like His beloved.

Set Free to Do What?

Let's now circle back to Galatians 5:1 where Paul says, "It is for freedom that Christ has set us free." We've already talked about what we have been set free *from*—the rigorous demands of the law. Now let's look at what we have been set free *to do*. This is precisely what Paul is getting at when he writes about this radical freedom again in Galatians 5:13–14:

> *It is absolutely clear that God has called you to a free life.*
> *Just make sure that you don't use this freedom as an excuse*
> *to do whatever you want to do and destroy your freedom.*
> *Rather, use your freedom to serve one another in love;*
> *that's how freedom grows. For everything we know about*
> *God's Word is summed up in a single sentence: Love others*
> *as you love yourself. That's an act of true freedom.*
> (MSG)

We have been set free to do *what*? Love! Not earn. Not perform. Not strive. Not prove. Not try harder. But to love. That is, in Paul's words, true freedom.

> We have been set free to *love!* Not earn. Not perform. Not strive. Not prove. Not try harder. But to love.

May I ask you a question? What emotion do those words evoke in you? Suspicion? Relief? Does it seem too good to be true? Or is it the very thing upon which you hang your hope? Perhaps it's all of the above, depending on the day or hour.

See, this is meant to feel like really good news, but to the doers and the overachievers, it can feel frustrating. (I might know a little something about that!)

For those of us who can't help but question, *"Are you really telling me that there isn't anything I can do to garner more of His love and pleasure?"* this might not feel like such good news at all.

In fact, as I began to discover this wild grace, I was skeptical, to say the least. My ego also took a hit. I didn't like the notion that all the striving I'd done to make God more pleased with me was in vain. I must have *something* to contribute. I think that's called pride. And rest assured, God is still faithfully working that out of me.

Apparently, God had to work pride out of King David as well, who writes in Psalm 51:16–17 (MSG):

> *Going through the motions doesn't please you, a flawless performance is nothing to you. I learned God-worship when my pride was shattered. Heart-shattered lives ready for love don't for a moment escape God's notice.*

141

Again, what we find here is that what pleases God is not a "flawless performance." He is pleased by our trust and faith in Him, and He is pleased by our obedience, *when* our obedience is a result of that faith and trust in His love for us (Hebrews 11:6). What pleases God is His Son, Jesus Christ. What pleases Him is a humble and repentant heart that pleads for mercy when sin entangles.

Accepting *that* gift pleases Him. And when we do, beautiful and mysterious things begin to happen in our lives and, therefore, in our parenting.

God Beckons Us to Freedom

Will you lean in and listen to God's voice beckoning you to freedom? God's promise to Israel in Isaiah 43 is His promise over our lives as well. Let it wash over you.

> *Do not be afraid. For I have bought you and made you free. I have called you by name. You are Mine! When you pass through the waters, I will be with you. When you pass through the rivers, they will not flow over you. When you walk through the fire, you will not be burned. The fire will not destroy you. For I am the Lord your God, the Holy One of Israel, Who saves you. I have given Egypt as pay for your life, and have traded Cush and Seba for you. You are of great worth in My eyes. You are honored and I love you.*
> (Isaiah 43:1–4 NLV)

If there is any iota of you that is still trying to earn God's affection and pleasure through your own goodness, and if you have yet to feel the grace of God deep in your bones, I'd like to invite you to personalize what you've just read in Isaiah. In fact, this invitation isn't just for those who are still trying to earn God's pleasure. It's for all of us. We need to be reminded repeatedly of the freedom for which Christ has set us free. So no matter where you are on the spectrum, will you join me in claiming this truth?

Lord, You have set me free. You have called me by name and I belong to you. I am of great worth in your eyes, Lord. I don't have to fear your rejection. I don't have to be afraid of losing your affection. You have saved me from proving I am worthy. You love me and you will never, ever forsake me.

Help me believe what you've promised to me and that what you say about me is true. Help me live like it's true, because it is.

CHAPTER 13

Our Struggle: God Wants Me to Prove My Love

God's Truth: God Calls Me to Repent and Rest in His Love

We're a very expressive family. We love to demonstrate our love. In words, in sticky notes, in physical affection, in interpretive dance. Okay, maybe not through interpretive dance. Actually, yes, through interpretive dance. Goofy is my thing. I digress. Anyhow, Hubby and I love finding creative ways to express our love to our boys.

Sometimes it's a note on the kitchen counter that greets them in the morning with, "You are so special. I know God could have chosen anyone in the whole wide world to be your mom, and I'm so happy He chose me."

Sometimes it's a sticky note in their lunch bag: "Be strong and courageous. God is with you and God is for you."

Sometimes it's an unexpected tickle attack that demonstrates "I enjoy you."

Sometimes it's a simple whisper in the ear that sounds like "I love who you are and I love who you're becoming." I most enjoy saying this to my boys when the day's been long and the struggle's been real. I find the hard days provide the most fertile soil to plant seeds of God's love.

Well, when we say to our two older boys, "I love you," they respond as you'd expect. They smile and sweetly say, "I love you too." Oh, what that does to my momma heart.

But when we tell Owen, our third son, that we love him, he's always had a unique response. He will very tenderly smile and respond, "I know." And then he will usually follow it up with an "I love you, too."

When Owen says those two simple words—"I know"—he blesses me with his confidence in my love. It melts my heart to know he trusts how very much he is loved by me. And it makes me think

> We bless Jesus with our confidence in His love for us.

that perhaps we bless Jesus with our confidence in His love for us. In fact, I know we do. As David writes in Psalm 147:11, "The Lord delights in those who fear him, who put their hope in his unfailing love" (NIV).

Who does the Lord delight in? Those who rarely sin and rebel? No. He delights in those who fear him. Now let's be clear—the expression "those who fear him" isn't referring to those who are petrified of Him. It doesn't mean "fear" as we would typically assume. God does not delight in us running and hiding, worrying that He is out to get us and punish us for our wrongdoing.

David is writing about *holy* fear—a fear that makes us stand in awe and wonder of God. A fear that makes us want to run toward Him, not away from Him, knowing that His arms are spread wide in welcome as we repent of our sin and receive His love. This kind of fear gives us a thirsty soul that can only be quenched by His presence. In other words, the Lord delights in us delighting in Him, and anchoring our hope in Christ's work to secure God's unfailing love for us.

When we read a passage such as 1 John 3:1 NIV, in which the apostle John writes, "See what great love the Father has lavished on us, that we should be called children of God! And that is what we are!" the Lord longs to hear us, in faith, respond, "I know."

Just as I love to hear my son say, "I know" when I tell him I love him, this passage, among countless others we've already read together, calls out for our confident response—*"I know!"*

"I Know" He Loves Me

I used to think that Jesus was pleased to see me working hard for His approval and love. It never occurred to me that I bless Him when I simply *believe* that He loves me as I am.

I know how heartbroken I would be if any of my boys thought they had to work for my love and approval—that my love for them was contingent on what they did or didn't do. I'd desperately want to assure them, "There is nothing you can do to make me love you less. And there is nothing you can do to make me love you more. *I love you just because I love you.* And that is never, ever going to change."

Similarly, Jesus delights in our "I know," in our trust, in our *belief*. In fact, He doesn't just delight in it. It's the very first command of His public ministry in the Gospel of Mark. Let's read it together:

One day Jesus came from Nazareth in Galilee, and John
baptized him in the Jordan River. As Jesus came up out of the
water, he saw the heavens splitting apart and the Holy Spirit
descending on him like a dove. And a voice from heaven said,
"You are my dearly loved Son, and you bring me great joy."
The Spirit then compelled Jesus to go into the wilderness,
where he was tempted by Satan for forty days. He was out
among the wild animals, and angels took care of him.
Later, after John was arrested, Jesus went into Galilee, where
he preached God's Good News. "The time promised by God
has come at last!" he announced. "The Kingdom of God is
near! Repent of your sins and believe the Good News!"
(Mark 1 9–16 NLT)

"Repent and believe" is His first command.

To understand the magnitude of what Jesus said here, we need to be clear on what repentance really is. Repentance is more than feeling sorry for our sin or regretting the consequences of it. It's a deep sorrow for wrongdoing that leads to an internal change of heart and mind. In fact, the word *repent* comes from the Greek word *metanoia*, which means "to have a change of heart."

Repent doesn't mean "try harder." It means "run to Jesus." Beg Him, by the power of His Holy Spirit, to change you from the inside out. It's what He came to do. The enemy tempts you to wallow in your mistakes, but Jesus beckons you to repent and rest in His righteousness.

> Repent doesn't mean "try harder." It means "run to Jesus."

We can approach Him with confidence in the knowledge that our shortcomings and sins do not shock or surprise Him. "God is greater than our heart and He knows everything," so "whenever our heart condemns us"—and it will—we must remember this: He wants us to *accept* our *acceptance* in Christ, and believe we remain His Beloved (1 John 3:20 ESV).

With Repentance Comes Rest

With belief and repentance comes rest—the rest I know you and I are both desperate for! This truth is highlighted by the prophet Isaiah, and let me tell you, this is one of the most convicting verses in the Bible for me. Isaiah writes:

> *This is what the Sovereign Lord, the Holy One of Israel,*
> *says: "In repentance and rest is your salvation, in quietness*
> *and trust is your strength, but you would have none of it."*
> (Isaiah 30:15 NIV)

Oh, how those last seven words pierce me: *"but you would have none of it."* How often I will have none of it. How often I'm content to offer a quick "sorry," brush my sins under the rug, and get back to the business of trying to do a better job of living the Christian life in my own strength.

But what an extraordinarily patient and faithful and loving God we have, as Isaiah goes on to demonstrate. "Yet," he writes, "the Lord longs to be gracious to you; therefore he will rise up to show you compassion" (30:18). And the prophet Micah expounds, He will "throw [our sin] into the depth of the ocean" (Micah 7:19 NLT).

When my heart needs to cry out in repentance, I turn to

Psalm 51. Though there are countless passages in Scripture that can guide us in repentance, this passage is one that always cracks me open to God.

In this passage, we find King David humbly crying out to God for forgiveness after Nathan confronted him about his adultery with Bathsheba. The depths of his sorrow and the burden of his guilt are palpable. I'd love to encourage you to pause here and read Psalm 51 in its entirety. (I'll wait!) Is it not breathtakingly beautiful? Here is just a portion of it for us to read together:

> *Have mercy on me, O God, because of your unfailing love.*
> *. . . For I recognize my rebellion; it haunts me day and night.*
> *. . . Purify me from my sins, and I will be clean; wash me,*
> *and I will be whiter than snow. . . . Create in me a clean*
> *heart, O God. . . . Renew a loyal spirit within me. Restore*
> *to me the joy of your salvation, and make me willing to*
> *obey you. . . . The sacrifice you desire is a broken spirit. You*
> *will not reject a broken and repentant heart, O God.*
> (NLT)

You and I have been personally invited to exchange striving and shame for repentance and rest. In Christ alone, we have a record of righteousness *and* the rest our souls crave. Restlessness will rule the hearts of those in pursuit of self-perfection. But rest will enfold the hearts of those who anchor their

> You and I have been personally invited to exchange striving and shame for repentance and rest.

identity in the perfection of Christ. Yes! Resting in Christ's work sets us free!

How Does God's Rest Impact Our Parenting?

Dear fellow mom, you and I are God's daughters, and we are *fiercely loved*. And we who are fiercely loved are empowered to love our children fiercely—fulfilling the new commandment of Christ:

So now I am giving you a new commandment: Love each other. Just as I have loved you, you should love each other. Your love for one another will prove to the world that you are my disciples. (John 13:34–35; see also 1 John 3:23 NLT)

Our ability to love our kids with the love of Christ—and fulfill this new commandment in our parenting—will be profoundly influenced by our willingness to rest in Jesus' love for us. He doesn't just love our lovable parts. He loves all of us, all of the time. Not just when we are obeying Him, trusting Him, and pulling this parenting thing off pretty well. But also when we are messing up again, losing our patience again, being unthankful again, or doing that "thing" we determined never to do again.

On the days when we don't feel the least bit lovely or lovable, we remain His beloved. We must trust the Word of God over the unrelenting critic in our head. We must make every untrue and rebellious thought captive to who God says we are in Christ! (2 Corinthians 10:5).

My friend, the price was paid and the point was made. *You. Are. Free!*

> The price was paid and the point was made. *You. Are. Free!*

While it is unfathomable to think that such a costly gift would be given to us with no strings attached, it is even more astounding to see how accepting God's unwavering and unconditional love changes everything about how we do life and how we lead our kids!

If we are living in guilt and shame over sins from our past, and if we are plagued by our inability to be close-to-perfect moms in the present, those guilt-ridden and shameful messages will overflow into our parenting. And we will fall deeper into despair over our inability to love our kids with the love of Christ.

But! If we are living in the freedom of God's grace, we will be empowered to raise children who also live in freedom. For the love that God pours into our hearts *enables us* to love and lead with His kind of love.

> *God is able to make all grace overflow to you so that, in all things and at all times, having all you need, you will overflow with every good work.*
> (2 Corinthians 9:8 MOUNCE)

Indeed, the grace we so generously receive will be the grace that we so generously give.

Are we ready to see the Good News come more fully alive

in our homes? It's time to turn to part 3 and discover how—in addition to grace being the overflow of our own hearts being anchored in grace—we can make every effort to establish a Gospel-centered pattern of parenting and implement practices that will make grace reverberate throughout our homes!

PART THREE

Parenting with Grace

CHAPTER 14

Who Am I?

Making the Gospel Central in Our Homes

We had one of *those* days. You know the kind I'm talking about—the kind where nobody is listening and everybody is disobeying, and I all too quickly unraveled with a temper tantrum of my own. Yes, that kind.

After I lost my temper, I gathered my boys on the couch and apologized to them. "I'm really sorry for getting so angry and letting my sinful nature win. I'm not excusing your behavior, and your consequences remain. But I *am* asking for your forgiveness for how I handled it. I didn't model God's patient and kind heart to you. Will you please forgive me?"

My boys graciously accepted my apology and went about their business. But my precious nine-year-old son Brennan snuggled closer into me on the couch and whispered in my ear, "Hey,

Mom, I don't think you have a sinful nature. I think you have a loving nature."

Brennan wanted to comfort me. He didn't want me feeling lousy about myself. That makes perfect sense from the perspective of a nine-year-old boy. He wanted to assure his momma that he loves her. In that beautiful moment, God opened the door for me to share the Gospel—again—with my son. It sounded something like this: "Buddy, that is so sweet of you. Thank you. But I want you to know that the bad news of my sinful nature always leads me to the good news of my sinless Savior who loved me and gave Himself for me."

> The bad news of my sinful nature always leads me to the good news of my sinless Savior who loved me and gave Himself for me.

I attempted to explain the complexity of the both/and to my son. I told him that my "sinful fallen nature" is only part of my story. That's not *all I am*. We are sinners. But our sin doesn't have the final word. God does. And because of what Jesus did for us, He calls us His deeply loved children. That is who I am! And knowing *that* is what frees me to be honest about my persistent sinful nature. And I assured him that my "loving nature" is always and only because of the love that Jesus Christ has first poured into me" (see John 1:12, Galatians 2:20, 1 John 3:17).

In response, my son gave me the perplexed look I often see when we have deep conversations about faith. It's the look that says, "I'm trying to understand. I really am!" So I assured him that it's okay to have questions and curiosity and even confusion. And I assured him we will keep talking about this. A lot.

Bad News/Good News

I've wrestled at great length with how to explain this both/and to our kids—that we are both sinful in the flesh and 100 percent righteous *in Christ*. And that because of Jesus, we are a "new creation" (2 Corinthians 5:17 ESV).

The bad news is that we carry inherited sin in our hearts because of the rebellion of Adam and Eve (Genesis 3, 8:21). From the very moment we are born, we have no shot at perfection or achieving a righteousness of our own—no chance whatsoever (Psalm 51:5, 58:3).

The Bible is clear on our human condition without the grace of God. Let's revisit the verses we read in Chapter 10 about our fallen nature:

- We are dead in our sin (Ephesians 2:1; Romans 5:12).
- There is no one who does good, not even one (Psalm 14:3).
- Whoever keeps the whole law but fails in one point has become accountable for all of it (James 2:10).
- Scripture has shut up all men under sin (Galatians 3:22).
- Every intent of the thoughts of men's hearts were only evil continually (Genesis 6:5).
- The heart is fooled more than anything else, and is very sinful. Who can know how bad it is (Jeremiah 17:9).
- Surely I was sinful at birth, sinful from the time my mother conceived me (Psalm 51:5).
- For all have sinned and fall short of the glory of God (Romans 3:23).

- And if we say we have no sin, we deceive ourselves and the truth is not in us (1 John 1:7–8).

And yet! The Good News is that we are simultaneously loved and accepted by God. Scripture assures us:

- You are fearfully and wonderfully made (Psalm 139).
- You are created in the very image of your Father (Genesis 1:27).
- You were chosen before the foundation of the world to be God's beloved, adopted, accepted, redeemed, and forgiven children (Ephesians 1:3–8).
- You are a King's kid (1 John 3:1).
- You're a friend of God (John 15:12–15).
- You're the apple of His eye (Psalm 17:8).
- You are delighted in and celebrated over (Zephaniah 3:17).
- You are an heir of God and co-heir with Christ (Romans 8:16–17).
- You are His *masterpiece,* created in Christ to do the good things He planned for you long ago (Ephesians 2:8–11).

The bad news/Good News is indeed a complicated thing to teach our children. And yet it's the most important teaching of all. Because, just as I told Brennan, the bad news of our sinful nature leads us directly to the Good News of Jesus who was "pierced for our rebellion, crushed for our sins. He was beaten so we could be whole. He was whipped so we could be healed.

All of us, like sheep, have strayed away. We have left God's paths to follow our own. Yet the Lord laid on him the sins of us all" (Isaiah 53:5–6 NLT).

The Good News is "To all who believed him and accepted him, he gave the right to become children of God. They are reborn— not with a physical birth resulting from human passion or plan, but a birth that comes from God" (John 1:12–13 NLT). And "because of his great love for us, God, who is rich in mercy, made us alive with Christ even when we were dead in transgressions—it is by grace you have been saved" (Ephesians 2:4–5 NIV).

Teaching the Whole Truth

I know it may feel overwhelming, intimidating, or even frightening to talk to our kids about sin because we worry it will hurt their self-confidence. We don't want our kids to feel badly about themselves, just as my precious Brennan didn't want me feeling badly about myself when I confessed my sinful nature. But God hasn't called us to grow our child's confidence in self. God doesn't want our children depending on their own goodness. He wants them looking to Christ for their goodness. *He wants them to live in freedom from trying to be good enough!* He wants them living in the assurance that He doesn't love them because they've been good enough. He loves them because they belong to Him!

> God doesn't want our children depending on their own goodness. He wants them looking to Christ for their goodness.

Jack Klumpenhower, in his fantastic book, *Show Them Jesus*, frames this well. He writes:

> Kids who trust in being good can't handle reminders of their sin. It destroys their self-confidence, precisely because it is confidence in self. For those who firmly trust in Jesus, even a hard look at their sin only makes them appreciate him more. The cure for kids who feel burdened by sin is not to ignore the topic (they feel the burden anyway, even if they aren't talking about it) but to administer large doses of the good news so that their trust in Jesus grows. We are sinners but no longer guilty, no longer unclean, no longer ashamed.[1]

What at first appears to be quite the conundrum is actually a marvelous mystery. The point of talking to our children about their sinful nature isn't to make them feel guilty about how bad they are. It's to make them exceedingly grateful for how good Jesus was for them. It's all grace. This is how we work with God to raise children who have a vibrant faith!

Do you remember the research we explored in part 1? It concluded, "The common thread that binds together almost every ministry-minded twenty-something is a home where the gospel was not peripheral but absolutely central, and ultimately operated from a framework of grace that held up the cross of Jesus as the basis for peace with God and forgiveness toward one another."[2]

The point of talking to our children about their sinful nature isn't to make them feel guilty about how bad they are. It's to make them grateful for how good Jesus was for them.

Well, moms, if we want to make the Gospel central in our homes and operate from a framework of grace, two things need to happen:

1. We have to speak honestly with our kids about who we are—in the flesh—before our holy God.
2. We have to give our children the Good News so they can see Jesus for who He *truly* is, and who they are *in* Him.

These two things go hand in hand. If we talk only about their sinful nature, we will leave them drowning in despair, and the song that will likely play on repeat in their heads is, "I am bad, I am bad, I always will be bad."

But if we talk only about how loved they are by God, we will lead them down the path of pride and ingratitude for Jesus. The song that will likely play on repeat in their head will sound more like, "I am good. All is love. I don't need a Savior."

Helping our children see the reality of their sinful nature is what will inspire them to fall in love with the One who takes great pleasure in transforming broken sinners into beloved children of God. *They are free!* Free to confess how sinful they are and free to celebrate how deeply loved they are in Christ.

Who Am I?

The foundation to making the Gospel central in our homes is helping our children answer the question "Who am I?" with the truth of God's Word. "Who am I?" is the single question

Henri Nouwen proposed that every human being is hounded by, and our children are no exception. We want them to be able to answer that question with: *"I am a completely known, fully accepted, and unconditionally loved child of God. I am His beloved."*

God fully knows every hair on our children's heads, every thought in their minds, and every dream in their hearts. But He also fully knows their sins and shortcomings and struggles and sorrows. And He spreads His arms wide open and welcomes them and accepts them at their best and at their worst. Impressing this Good News on the hearts of our kids will empower them to say, *"I am loved simply because I am His. He loves me simply because He loves me."*

Why is this so important? Because everything our children say and do, desire and love, long for and dream about, will be influenced by the answer to this one question: Do they know the wholehearted love of God that is *already* theirs *because of* Jesus Christ?

Remember Who Holds Their Hearts

Now, let's pause here, because I think we need to acknowledge a hard truth: *No matter how hard we try,* we don't hold the power to control what our child's heart believes. We can no more make them see their need for a Savior than we can convince them how deeply loved they are by God. We can't make them accept their acceptance in Christ or see themselves through God's lens of grace. Only the Holy Spirit can do that.

Only the Holy Spirit can enlighten our children's hearts to see that their righteous status before God was secured in Christ (see Ephesians 1:18).

What we can do, however, is give them the Good News found in God's Word. May we never, ever underestimate its power to penetrate our child's innermost being. "For the word of God is alive and

> Only the Holy Spirit can enlighten our children's hearts to see that their righteous status before God was secured in Christ.

powerful. It is sharper than the sharpest two-edged sword, cutting between soul and spirit, between joint and marrow. It exposes our innermost thoughts and desires" (Hebrews 4:12 NLT).

We have the privilege and responsibility of feeding their hearts with the Good News *every day*. Because they, like us, will forget it *every day*. Let us not forget that the enemy is working tirelessly to feed our children lies. He wants them to wallow in their weaknesses and doubt the love of God. He will never stop trying to convince them that God will give up on them and that God's grace will eventually run out on them. So we must feed them the Gospel.

But! As we do, let it bring us great relief to remember that God longs for our children to know the fullness of His love even more than we do. So we are free to give them the Good News in God's Word, show them with our own lives what it means to live by grace, pray that the Holy Spirit will open their eyes to their true selves—radically loved, forgiven, and treasured children of God—and then rest in God's sovereignty and grace.

Now, if feeding the Gospel to your children—in moments

big and small—is foreign to you or you simply struggle with how to integrate the Gospel into your daily parenting, hang in there. That is exactly what this section is all about. Be assured we are going to see how to do this in very practical daily ways!

But as we move toward these answers, there is another question that our kids desperately need to know the answer to: "Is who I am good enough?"

CHAPTER 15

Is Who I Am Good Enough?

Freeing Our Children from the Pressure of Performance

A young mother of two daughters was sharing some of her parenting struggles with me. She spoke of how over-whelmed she felt in the early days of parenting when she was dis-covering how differently each of her children were wired, how foreign their personalities were from hers, and how ill equipped she felt to parent them. At her wits' end, she asked for advice from a mentor whom she admired, whose own children were adults. But rather than being quick to offer advice, her mentor replied with a question. "What if you just let them be who they are?"

Letting our children "be who they are" is probably one of the biggest challenges we face. Not piling our expectations onto them. Not living our lives through them. Not expecting them to do things the way we would do them. Not passing on to them the pressure we feel. Finding the right balance between affirming who they are while still encouraging them to grow. Teaching them to give their best without making them feel like they must be the best at everything.

Letting our children "be who they are" is probably one of the biggest challenges we face.

For example, I recently overheard two mothers lamenting about the pressure their children had recently been under during the college application process. Toward the end of the conversation, one woman said to the other, "Thank God she got into the college of my, oops, I mean, her choice." They both giggled, and my heart broke for the pressure I assume her child must have felt. But before I could tuck my pointed finger back into the palm of my hand, God invited me to take an honest look at what undue pressure my children might be feeling because of me. Ouch.

Attaching Our Worth to Our Child's Works

There is so much that we want for these kids that we love so much, and there is very little that will stop us from ensuring they achieve their full potential and purpose. Sometimes that's a good thing. Sometimes it is not.

Heeding the advice of the well-known proverb, "Prepare the child for the path, not the path for the child," is a good thing. But, living vicariously through our kids and shackling our identities to their success or failure—not so much.

Have you ever been tempted to attach your worth to your child's works? Have you been tempted to believe that your child's bad choices makes you a "bad" mom and your child's good choices makes you a "good" mom. Or maybe you've been more than just tempted. Maybe you've actually anchored *who you are* in *what your children do*. I certainly have.

Now, listen. Of course it is good and right to be proud of the good choices our kids make and to be on our knees in prayer over the not-so-good choices our kids make. But if our *worth* is anchored to our child's choices, their good choices will inflate our heads and their bad choices will deflate our hearts. And that is just no way to live.

> If our *worth* is anchored to our child's choices, their good choices will inflate our heads and their bad choices will deflate our hearts. And that is just no way to live.

More important, if our worth is anchored to our child's choices, we better believe they feel the weight of it. It's a pressure, a burden that they are not designed to carry. It's too heavy. It will crush them. It *is* crushing them.

Why Are Our Kids So Miserable?

There is a reason teenagers are now the most stressed-out age group in the United States, according to the American Psychology Association's 2013 Stress in America survey. Sadly, we have never seen a generation of kids who are more miserable than this one.

Researchers have a slew of theories for why we are seeing so much misery among kids, but if you guessed that how we parent is one of them, you're correct. A recent article entitled "Why Are Our Kids So Miserable?" reported:

> Maybe driven by love, or perhaps a sense of paranoia, some parents are veering toward micro-managing our kids' every mini-success (while extolling the virtues of failure).
>
> We help with the science project, edit the college essay, advocate for the better grade, and apologize on the playground when little Lucy won't share the way we grown-ups think she should share. We set lots of rules for our kids, and wonder why they can't set their own.
>
> Parents also play a critical role in setting those high expectations. At the upper end of the socioeconomic spectrum, we may be too evolved to push them toward the Ivy League, but we certainly want them to try their hardest—at everything: school, music, soccer, piano, judo, street dance. We say it's not all about winning, but celebrate winning in spades.[1]

The Pressure We Put on Our Kids

The evidence is irrefutable. Kids are overwhelmed by the pressure to perform. And a lot of this pressure comes from us, their parents. We might do it unintentionally, but there's no denying that most of us are doing it in some form or fashion.

And it starts early. Take, for example, the grocery store scenario. We are mortified when our kids throw a temper tantrum in the checkout lane. Why? Because that must mean we're a bad mom. It must mean we haven't done everything we know to do to raise children who are well behaved and self-controlled. Right? It's a silly example but worth noting how we, from very early on, need our kids to look awesome because we think that makes *us* look awesome.

Or how about the athletic field? There are few places we see parents piling the pressure onto their kids more than they do there. Coaches and parents alike question the refs and umps, scream at the players, and throw profanity around like confetti. We've kinda lost our minds, and our kids crack under the pressure.

Could it be that we need our kids to succeed because that means *we're* succeeding? Do we need our kids to be "good enough" because it means that we parents are "good enough?" Do we need our child to get "student of the month" because that must mean we are "parent of the month"?

> Do we need our kids to be "good enough" because it means that we parents are "good enough?"

Of course, some kids are just more prone to perfection seeking than others. Such kids tend to create their own pressure, even if their parents are actively trying to relieve it. But often, we parents play a role in the pressure our kids feel, so we have to be willing to take an honest look at how we pile our own pressure onto our kids.

See, we parents aren't the only ones linking accomplishment to acceptance and success to significance. Our kids are attempting to answer the question, *Is who I am enough?* by:

- how well they perform on the field
- how much they excel in school

- how many likes they get on their Instagram feed
- how well they behave for us
- how well they follow the commandments in the Bible

Our kids are riddled with anxiety from their over-committed schedules. They are depressed and fearful and overmedicated, and it's hurting them—and sometimes literally killing them.[2]

The primary message our children receive is that they'd better be the best at everything, and this leaves them afraid to reveal their inadequacies and insecurities—and hiding behind the best version of themselves.

It's a vicious cycle, leaving parents and children alike longing for what all our hearts most crave:

- *to be known*—truly and deeply known
- *to be accepted*—for who they are, not who they wish they were
- *to be loved*—with no strings attached

> The primary message our children receive is that they'd better be the best at everything, and this leaves them afraid to reveal their inadequacies and insecurities.

And guess what? This isn't just happening to kids outside the church. No, it's happening inside of it.

What We're Seeing in Our Churches

Recently, after speaking on this topic at a national parenting conference, I met a woman who came forward to share her experience of this epidemic. She is a youth worker in a large church, and she said that the number one issue she sees in the kids she ministers to is that they believe their *behavior* makes them more lovable or less lovable to their parents.

And because parents serve as a template for how children perceive God, the kids in her ministry link their good and bad behavior to how God feels about them—assuming He feels good about them when they do good and bad when they do bad. Her youth group, she explained, is full of kids who don't feel "good enough."

But we aren't seeing this in just our youth. Sally Lloyd-Jones, author of the *Jesus Storybook Bible*, says that when she goes into churches to speak to children, she asks them two questions. First, she asks, "Who thinks you have to be good for God to love you?" The children tentatively raise their hands. Second, she asks, "And how many of you think that if you aren't good, God will stop loving you?" The children again raise their hands.

Sally explains, "These are children in Sunday schools who know the Bible stories. These are children who probably know all the right answers and yet somehow missed the most important thing of all: in spite of everything, no matter what, whatever it cost him, God won't ever stop loving His children."[3]

My fellow mom, the Good News for children who don't feel good enough is this:

- If you ever had a shot at being *enough*, then Jesus died for nothing.
- Jesus was more than *enough* on your behalf.
- Jesus loved you *enough* to leave heaven, live a perfect life for you, and ultimately lay down His life for you.

When we give our children this Good News, they no longer have to question, "Is who I am enough?" Now they have an anthem: "Jesus is my enough."

This Good News frees our children from searching for significance in all the wrong places. Because, ultimately, isn't that what they—and we—are doing?

When we ask (as in the previous chapter) "Who am I?" and now, "Is who I am good enough?" what we are ultimately doing is searching for significance.

Searching for Significance

Now, if you've lived long enough, you already know this to be true. Our search for significance in anything or anyone other than Jesus will *always* leave us longing for more. It—*whatever it is*—will never be enough. From our youngest days to our dying days, we will relentlessly chase more.

> Our search for significance in anything or anyone other than Jesus will *always* leave us longing for more.

Whatever we chase, it will ultimately disappoint, maybe even devastate, all depending on how dependent we are on that person or thing to provide us with what only Jesus can provide. We chase after:

- the first-place medal
- the boyfriend
- the popular circle of friends
- the impeccable report card
- the Ivy League school
- the dream job
- the fit body
- the big bank account
- the fancy car
- the husband
- the 2.5 kids
- the white picket fence
- the extravagant vacations
- the social media attention
- the promotion
- the praise

Whether we like it or not, whether we realize it or not, our children are watching. We can rest assured that our chase for significance impacts our children.

But the same could be said if our souls are satisfied in Jesus. When our lives demonstrate the truth that our significance is not based on what we do or what we have, but on what's been done for

> Rest assured, our chase for significance impacts our children. But the same could be said if our souls are satisfied in Jesus.

us *by* Jesus and what we have *in* Jesus, our children will witness the fruit of freedom in our lives. What makes us—and our children—significant is not what we have but whose we are!

A Better Way!

Friend, I am typing this with all the conviction my small fingers can muster. There is a better way! A way to freedom. A way out of the vicious cycle of performance and into the unforced rhythms of God's grace (Matthew 11:28–30 MSG). How do I know? Well, because God's Word tells me so. And I also know because this is my story. This is the road I have traveled and the road I continue to travel.

For too long, I lived under the self-imposed pressure of unrealistic expectations, and I therefore put that same pressure on my kids. I didn't feel "good enough" to be a recipient of God's goodness. I didn't feel good enough to raise the children God had entrusted to me. And I had a five-year-old little boy who was walking on eggshells around me because he was afraid to make one wrong move and confirm he wasn't good enough to meet the unrealistic expectations of perfection I'd put on him. Had God not intervened, it was only a matter of time before the pressure made its way to our three-year-old, our one-year-old, and our fourth son, who came along seven years later.

I passed the pressure down. There's no way around it. When the "not enough" penetrates our lives, it plagues our parenting. Even though that's the last thing we want.

We want our kids to know with utter certainty that when they fail and when they succeed, when they obey and when they rebel, when they do lovable things and when they do unlovable things, when they do "good stuff" and when they do "bad stuff" that everything they need to be "enough" before God, they already have in Jesus (Philippians 4:19).

We want them to feel what we ourselves long to feel. Safe. Safe to take off their masks and let down their guard. Safe to be as fragile as they feel, trusting they will remain loved just as they are, for exactly who they are.

When the internal and external voices whisper lies to our children like, "You're insignificant. You're not enough. You're not measuring up. You are a disappointment," we want them to know, deep in their souls: *The only One who gets to define you is the One who created you and redeemed you, and He calls you beloved.*

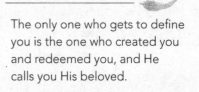

The only one who gets to define you is the one who created you and redeemed you, and He calls you His beloved.

Well, my fellow mom, our ability to give our kids what we want to give them begins with this: by "letting the truth of our [own] belovedness become enfleshed in everything we think, say, or do."[4]

Easier said than done, I know. Oh, trust me, I know. And yet learning to walk in freedom from the pressure of performance and proving our "enough-ness" is how we lead our kids in doing the same. Indeed, more is caught than taught.

Let's keep that close in mind as we venture into the next chapter. Ready?

• CHAPTER 16 •

Broken Together

Giving Our Children Permission to Be
Honest about Their Weaknesses

I was sitting at the kitchen counter, typing away on my computer, when my son, Cal, came up from behind me, threw his arms around my neck, and asked, "Hey, Mom! Whatcha doing?"

"Hey, love!" I replied with a big smile. Sometimes just the very sight of my boys makes my heart skip a beat. "I'm speaking at a women's conference next week and I'm working on my talk."

"Are you going to talk about what you always talk about?" he asked as he leaned over my computer to read the screen.

I laughed. "Well, I don't know. What do you think I always talk about?"

He responded without hesitation. "How much you need Jesus."

Oh, my heart.

I put my arm around his waist and pulled him close. "I am,

buddy. That is exactly what I am going to talk about. How much I need Jesus and how grateful I am for His grace."

He kissed my forehead. "Cool. Love ya, Mom. I'm gonna go play soccer in the backyard." And just like that, he was off.

As I watched Cal kick the soccer ball around the backyard with his brothers, I became overwhelmed with gratitude for how far the Lord has brought us as a family, and how free He has made me to be real with my kids about my need for Him.

It hasn't always been this way for us.

As I've mentioned before, I eagerly anticipated parenthood with the expectation that I would make very few mistakes, have little regret, and raise little people who loved God very well. Maybe you also thought that's how it would go before little people invaded your home and reality hit the fan?

I should tell you, my excessively high expectations were born in a heart that really loved Jesus. A lot. The problem was, that heart was struggling to believe Jesus still loved me in the aftermath of my divorce. And my inability to be a perfect mom only compounded my shame.

> Because I was not willing to be honest about how much I was struggling, I suffered in silence.

I remember feeling so alone in my feelings of defeat and failure in those early days. I wouldn't dare share my "humanity" with my friends—much less, my kids. My hubby was the only one privy to my desperation. On countless nights, he would come home from work to find me curled up on the couch, crying a river, and cracking under the pressure. Yes, I had extraordinary friends who faithfully walked alongside me in those days. But because I was not willing to be honest about how much I was struggling, I mostly suffered in silence.

The painful belief that I wasn't "good enough" was confirmed on those late nights alone on the couch, and shame seeped deeper into the crevices of my heart. I "knew" God was disappointed in my inability to be all I longed to be for my kids, and it was only a matter of time before my kids would call my bluff.

Each night I promised God I'd do better tomorrow, but I'll bet you know how tomorrow looked. A lot like the day before. My "trying harder" didn't get me very far.

Whether you are the momma of a two-year-old or a thirty-two-year-old, I am going to guess that you, too, may be struggling in some areas of your parenting right now, and you don't love the idea of your weaknesses being on display for your children to see.

So the question begs, *How do we move from trying to hide our weaknesses and struggles and shortcomings to being okay with our children being privy to them?* Well, I *think* our answer—or at least one of our answers—lies in this:

> Our weaknesses can be used by God for His good purpose.

We accept that our brokenness and weakness can be used by God for His good purpose. A God-given and God-glorifying purpose in our parenting. This is no small thing!

Our Weakness and God's Strength

We see this so beautifully demonstrated in the life of the apostle Paul. Though he wasn't trying to raise tiny people into godly adults in the twenty-first century, he was commissioned to spread the Gospel of Christ to the first-century world after persecuting Christians—even having some put to death. Talk about God calling, forgiving, equipping, and using the most unlikely. That gives me serious hope for all the insecurities and inadequacies in my parenting.

In 2 Corinthians 12:7–8, we find Paul pleading with God to take away an affliction (precisely, a "thorn in my flesh," Paul writes) that reveals his human weaknesses. Scripture does not reveal the exact nature of Paul's affliction—whether it is physical, psychological, or situational—and, quite honestly, I think we're better off for it. Perhaps we'd focus more on the weakness Paul's affliction reveals than on what it's meant to accomplish in his life.

Well, rather than respond to Paul's pleading by removing the affliction, God said to Him, "My grace is all you need. My power works best in weakness" (2 Corinthians 12:9).

Can we just sit with that for a minute? We will get to how Paul responds in a moment, but first can we put ourselves in Paul's shoes and think about how we'd respond to God's answer? I'm pretty confident I would have said something along the lines of, "God, thank You for Your grace. I appreciate that. I really do. But I don't think You heard me right. I don't want affliction. I don't like feeling weak. I want to be awesome. I want to be strong. I want to be . . . self-sufficient. Oh, right. I guess what I'm saying, Lord, is that I don't want to need You or have to rely on You. I'd rather *be* You."

Thankfully, that's not how Paul responds. Instead, he says:

So now I can be glad to boast about my weaknesses,
so that the power of Christ can work through
me. When I am weak, I am strong.
(2 Corinthians 12:10)

What hope does this give us for our parenting?

The Lord's gracious assurance to Paul is the very same assurance He gives to you and to me: "My grace is all you need. My power works best in your weakness." So, just like the apostle Paul, we can boldly respond: "Now I can be glad to be honest with my children about my weaknesses, so that the divine power of Christ can work through me in my parenting. For when I can confess I am weak, then I am finally strong."

Being honest about our weaknesses keeps us parenting from a posture of humility, and it keeps us reliant on God. Humble and reliant. Exactly where He wants us! Oh, the sweet freedom I have found in knowing that my weaknesses give way to God's strength. That my weaknesses point my children away from their flawed mom and straight to their flawless Savior. He's the One I want their trust and hope set upon, not me.

Dear fellow mom, you don't have to be ashamed of your weakness and your need for Christ. He loves to meet you and strengthen you and glorify Himself through you in that place, by His grace!

You are free! Free to be honest about your weakness with your children.

> You don't have to be ashamed of your weakness and your need for Christ. He loves to meet you and strengthen you and glorify Himself through you in that place, by His grace!

Now, before we move on, I want to share something with you about this passage that I'd missed for so long. Said simply, weakness, as Paul is describing it, is different than sin. However, our weaknesses often lead us to sin. For example, my short temper (weakness) leads me to come down too hard on my kids (sin). My exhaustion (weakness) leads me to be selfish with my kids (sin). My lack of joy (weakness) leads me to parent with a critical spirit (sin). Without the divine power of Christ working through my weakness, my weakness leads to sin. But with the divine power of Christ comes obedience. Therefore, as we travel through this chapter together, we will talk about both weakness and sin, because, ultimately, what we want is for our children to be able to be honest about *both*.

Permission to Be Broken

In 2015, Casting Crowns released a stunning song entitled, "Broken Together." I can only imagine the number of marriages that have been healed and restored through the lyrics.

They sing, "Maybe you and I were never meant to be complete. Could we just be broken together?"

This song speaks to the ridiculously high expectations we put on one another to be what only Jesus can be for us. And it encourages us to hold on to hope as we remember one another's humanity, walk alongside one another in humility, and fight for healing. What I love about this song is that it isn't just for marriage. It's for life. It's for our friendships. It's for our workplace. It's for, yes, even our parenting. We must learn how to walk alongside our children in brokenness—we must learn *to be bro-*

> When we are honest about our brokenness, it gives our children permission to be honest about theirs.

ken together. And here's the beautiful thing about being broken together. When we are honest about our brokenness, it gives our children permission to be honest about theirs. This "permission" is really (really!) important.

If we don't demonstrate for our children—with our own lives—that our brokenness does not keep us from living meaningful, purposeful, abundant lives, they will hide their weakness, pain, and disappointment for fear that it will make them seem less valuable and lovable. We are the broken ones. He was the One who was willing to be broken so that we could one day be made whole. And being tender toward our child's brokenness flows from remembering our own.

So let's look at seven ways we can give our children permission to be honest about their weakness and brokenness, and live in freedom!

1. A Home of Confession, Not Perfection

Creating a home of confession, not perfection, means creating a place where—when we fail and the Holy Spirit does the convicting and sweet work in our hearts—we can run to Jesus, repent, and receive forgiveness *alongside* our children. This is how we raise kids who confess sin willingly and repent sincerely. Isn't that what we want for them? We want our children to be free from carrying secrets and suffering in silence—because this is where shame festers. We want them to be free to speak what sometimes feels like the unspeakable in a *safe place*. Right? Well, if we want to have a home like that, we need to go first. We take the lead. We let them see that *we* are free to confess our weaknesses and brokenness because we have a Savior who loves and welcomes the weak and forgives the broken.

> If we want our children to confess sin willingly and repent sincerely, we need to go first.

In fact, we become more of who our children need us to be, not in our growing awareness of how strong and good we are, but in our humble confession of how weak and broken we are, and how strong and good Jesus is for us—as we humbly say, *"I get it."*

2. "I Get It"

Three little words. But, oh, so profound.

When we come alongside our kids in their struggles and are willing to regularly say, "I get it," our kids will be set free from feeling like they must perform for us or get it all right to have our love or win our approval.

Let me give you an example through a story a grandmother recently shared with me. She said, "Our five-year-old grandson got frustrated with a computer game he was playing on the tablet that I bought him for Christmas—and he threw it on the floor! I told him in no uncertain terms not to do that, but I also sat him on my lap and said, 'I get it' and told him how frustrated I get with my tablet and computer. This simple phrase has made a big impact on how I relate to my little ones. Saying 'I get it' reminds us that we're in this together—we share the same sin and the same Savior."

I could very much resonate with her story. Let me give you a personal example.

3. "Me, Too"

I remember it like it was yesterday. A friendly game of backyard soccer between our boys turned into a screaming punching match. I usually let them work these things out on their own, but I could tell this was going nowhere good, and fast.

I ran barefoot out the back door, yanked one son off the other, and before I knew it, words of shame shot out of my mouth and straight into my son's heart.

"Who does that? What kind of boy hurts his brother like that?"

I knew immediately what my words had just done to my son's spirit, and my heart split open.

With the saddest eyes I've ever seen, my son looked up at me and whispered back through tears, "I guess someone like me."

This happened during the time I was just beginning to discover and surrender to God's grace for me. And so, in that moment, I knew: *I was living out the very shame I was living in.* And conviction hit me to the core.

By the mere grace of God, I fell to my knees so I could be eye to eye with my guy. I was already crying when I whispered back, *"Me too, baby, me too."* Someone like Mommy does something like that, too. I just let my anger win, too. I am so sorry, I was wrong for saying that to you. Will you please forgive me?"

With our arms wrapped around each other, we cried and we

prayed. We sought forgiveness, and we thanked God for loving us enough to give us Jesus.

After we wiped our tears away, my son got up, went to his brother, and sought forgiveness. I didn't have to tell him what to do. His heart was convicted and broken and healed by the Good News of Jesus.

See, my son's actions required correction and consequences, not condemnation. When we throw shame at our children's failures, we create hopelessness in them. But grace! Grace inspires hope. Grace affirms that, because of Jesus, there is absolutely nothing that can make us unlovable to God.

> Remembering grace transforms our message of "How could you?" into "Me, too!"

Remembering the grace that God has freely given us in Jesus Christ enables us to parent from a "broken together" place. Remembering grace transforms our message of "How could you?" into "Me, too!"

4. The Cross between Us

How do we remember our own brokenness in those heated moments? Well, I am a visual person. Tell me something, I forget it. Show me something, it's with me for life.

So what I have found to be incredibly helpful is literally envisioning a cross between my child and me. Shame and anger and fear tactics can't penetrate the Cross. If the Cross of Christ is between my child and me, there are only two ways to get to the other side. I either go around the Cross and discipline in my sinful nature, or I go through the Cross and discipline in grace.

5. Correction, Not Condemnation

So . . . if I had paused just long enough to put the Cross between my son and me that day in the backyard—if I had paused just long enough to remember my own daily sin and need for Jesus—my response would have looked so different. I would have been firm but gentle. I would have corrected him but not condemned him. I would have done what God does with us.

So often, we chase after an immediate behavioral response from our kids, when what we really want is a long-term transformed-heart response.

> If I had paused just long enough to put the Cross between my son and me, I would have corrected him but not condemned him.

And a transformed-heart response is only accomplished through understanding that the Cross is the ultimate act of love. This sacrifice is what kindles and inspires our love for God and our desire to obey His word. Putting the Cross between us— seeing our children through the lens of the self-giving love of Christ—teaches us to correct rather than condemn, and it transforms our experience with our children. It allows us to be broken together. This is how we make our homes a place of warmth and welcome.

6. Family Warmth

As long as we have a "warm" relationship with our kids, we have potential for influence. In fact, I recently read an insightful article by Kara Powell, at Fuller Youth Institute, regarding the results of a comprehensive study of relational dynamics in more than three hundred families spanning thirty-five years. The study found that *family warmth* is correlated with faith transmission more than any other relational factor—including amount of contact between the generations, the type of contact, and the number of children in the family. But there's more. The study also found that it's not *our* perception of warmth that matters most. It's *theirs.*[1]

Family warmth occurs when our children feel accepted just as they are. When a strong sense of belonging permeates the homes. When we welcome them in their weakness, rather than withdraw from them. When, as Kara Powell noted, not just our words, but our tone of voice and body language, emit warmth. Those last two habits—tone of voice and body language—were very convicting to read. Too often it's not my words that are the issue. It's my tone of voice or body language that builds walls between my kids and me. But here's the good news. It's never too late to change the temperature in our homes!

> Family warmth occurs when we welcome our children in their weakness, rather than withdraw from them. And it's never too late to change the temperature in our homes!

7. Gracious Rescue

Several years ago, I stumbled upon an interview with author Paul Tripp called "Grace Liberates Our Parenting." The title of the interview caught my attention because, well, who doesn't want to be liberated in their parenting? While the entire interview was full of incredible wisdom, one line has never left me. In fact, it has stayed in the forefront of my mind ever since. Tripp said, "All of parenting is a gracious rescue."

And he explained it this way:

> In a moment of correction and discipline, the whole thing that's moving in my heart is rescue. It's not, "You know what? I don't need to deal with this. Do you know what I do for you? Come on!" It's, "I understand what's going on with you because I'm a rebel sinner like you are. I understand why you hate authority. I understand why you want to rule your world. I understand your shocking selfishness or self-righteousness, and if today, in just one small step, I could be an instrument of God's rescuing you from you, I would be so delighted." It's a happy experience that is meant for the child.[2]

Did you ever imagine that correction and discipline could be a happy experience for you and your child?

Parenting as a "gracious rescue" means coming alongside our children in grace rather than coming down on them with shame. Rather than responding to their sin with shock, we respond with God's shocking love. And whether we choose grace or shame will have a significant impact on our relationship with our children — and on our children's spirit.

In fact, the most sacred space to demonstrate God's love is in our children's failure. God demonstrated His love to us at our worst. To reflect His heart, we need to do the same with our children. We must remember our own brokenness, and love them through theirs to make the Good News central in our homes.

> The most sacred space to demonstrate God's love is in our children's failure.

CHAPTER 17

Everyday Grace

Answering Common Questions
about Giving Our Kids Grace

"Mom, come on. Give us some grace! Pleeeeassse!"
That was my son Brennan's plea after I disciplined
my boys for the way they were treating each other on a Saturday
evening in the backyard. His request reflects a common misun-
derstanding about what it means to parent with grace. But rather
than tell you how I responded, how about we work together to
remember what grace *actually* is, and then answer some common
questions about how we parent with it. My hope is that not only
will my response to Brennan's plea be self-evident, but we will
also discover that more than anything else, parenting with grace
is the overflow of our own lives being rooted in and strengthened
by grace.

In this chapter, I've identified ten of the most common questions parents ask about parenting with grace. But to give a meaningful answer to each of them, you should know up front that this chapter is longer than the others. But hang in there with me, as I believe we'll find this exercise well worth it. The ten questions are:

1. What is grace?
2. What is "parenting with grace"?
3. How can we balance grace and discipline?
4. Is there a place for anger in our discipline?
5. Is it ever too late to give my kids grace?
6. Is it ever too early to give my kids grace?
7. What is the language of grace?
8. What is the language of shame?
9. What if my kids take advantage of grace?
10. *When* will we see the fruit of grace?

Now, as we dive into these questions, I want to tell you again—I by *no means* have all the answers. A challenging and complicated situation with my son, *just last night*, reminded me of this reality! There is so much I don't know and so much I still have to discover. In the words of Bob Goff, "I'm still an amateur at grace."

I am learning alongside you, dear mom. But I do want to share with you some of the things God has been teaching me through His Word and through other wise moms who have gone before me.

1. What Is Grace?

This is a big question on which all the others rest. We have to be clear on what grace actually is. I think we may be best served by looking, first, at what grace is not.

- Grace is not God looking at our sin and ignoring it or excusing it.
- Grace is not a free pass to sin or do as we please.
- Grace is not the absence of rules, boundaries, consistency, consequences, or discipline.
- Grace does not make obedience optional.

Grace *is* the unearned and undeserved favor of God. It is the means by which God saves, sustains, sanctifies, and strengthens us in the person and work of Jesus Christ. So, let's personalize that.

Grace is God looking at our sin—the gravity and magnitude of it—and out of His great love, choosing to give us Jesus to atone for it. This is how we know what love is: "Jesus Christ laid down His life for us" (1 John 3:16 NIV).

Grace has no frown face. It has no pointed finger. It has no crossed arms. It has no limits or conditions. In fact, grace with conditions isn't grace at all.

Grace is God's arms spread wide to us—at our very best and at our very worst moments.

Grace is outrageous forgiveness of our outrageous sin, given freely to us *while*, not *after*, we were still covered in the stench of sin.

Grace is pure, unfathomable, undeserved, unconditional love.

And that is only scratching the surface of grace. We could

spend the rest of our time together trying to describe the indescribable.

But we'll move on and see how God's grace translates to parenting.

2. What Is "Parenting with Grace"?

Again, let's start by identifying what parenting with grace is not.

- It is not ignoring or excusing our children's sin.
- It is not turning a blind eye to their behavior, or giving them a free pass to sin or do as they please.
- It is not the absence of establishing rules, boundaries, consistency, consequences, or discipline in our parenting.
- It does not make obedience optional for our children.

Then, what *is* parenting with grace? It is weaving the Good News of Jesus Christ *into* how we establish our authority, require obedience, train, and discipline our kids.

> Parenting with grace means weaving the Good News of Jesus Christ into how we establish our authority, require obedience, train, and discipline our kids.

It is reflecting God's heart of unconditional love and forgiveness when we address our children's sin and weaknesses.

It is remembering that when God disciplines us, His purpose isn't to show us who's boss.

It is recognizing that an angry tone and a shameful message will not convict our children's hearts and inspire obedience. Rescue and redirect.

Parenting from a framework of grace means relating to our children the same way that God relates to us.

3. How Can We Balance Grace and Discipline?

Now let's apply this understanding of grace to what seems to be the most pressing question we moms have about parenting with grace, and that is: "How can it be balanced with discipline?"

But knowing what we know now, can we agree that the better question is "How can I weave grace into my discipline?" Because grace and discipline aren't opposing principles to be balanced.

Grace is unconditional love woven into our words and actions when we discipline our kids.

Grace *in* discipline says, "You disobeyed me, and because I love you, I will give you consequences. I can't change your heart. Only God can do that. But I can help you learn from your mistakes and pray you make wise choices in the future."

> Grace in discipline is *corrective* and *instructional,* and it is for our child's *good.*

Grace in discipline is *corrective* and *instructional,* and it is for our child's *good.* It never uses shame or fear to accomplish its purpose. We want our kids to understand that the commandments and promises of Christ are *gifts* we give them—gifts that set them free to live into the purpose for which they were so wonderfully created.

For example, our boys were recently fighting over who punched who first, and who said what mean thing to who last. When I found them fighting in their "man cave," they all had different stories.

I did everything I know I'm not supposed to do. I threatened to take things they loved away. I got mad. I demanded the truth. And of course, none of that worked. They continued to argue and point fingers. Until I reminded them of grace.

I said, "Boys, I want you to be honest so you don't carry the guilt that comes with lying. And I want you to remember that whatever you did wrong has already been forgiven and paid for in Jesus. Ask God to give you a heart that desires honesty. *This is not a house of perfection, but confession.*"

I am by no means suggesting that this is a formula that "works" every time. Grace is not a formula. But grace often frees my kids to confess the things that fear or shame were preventing them from disclosing. That's what grace does.

I'm also not saying they don't receive consequences. Of course they do. Our children must learn that there are, and always will be, consequences to their actions—whether they be good consequences for good decisions or painful consequences for poor choices. So whenever possible, I choose logical consequences—ones that correlate with the behavior that requires discipline.

Our kids need—and want!—us to be consistent in this. Our two-year-old and our seventeen-year-old *need* us to establish healthy boundaries and be consistent with them! They may not know it. And they'll definitely never admit it. Right? I mean, when was the last time your child came to you and said, "Hey Mom, I really need you to be consistent with boundaries and consequences so I know I can count on you and learn to rely on God to make wise choices in the future!" Exactly! Me neither. But indeed, they need us to say what we mean and mean what we say. (Though let us not confuse consistent with stringent. If we overreact and give them a consequence that doesn't fit the crime, or if we are unreasonable when they want to explain their actions, or we are inflexible in a situation that could have used a little mercy, it's okay for us to back up and say, "I got that wrong and I want to make it right.")

Even so, we must remember that clear rules, consistent boundaries, and logical consequences may change our children's outward behavior in the short term, but they certainly won't lead them to repentance or bring lasting transformation of their hearts.

As we've discussed before, we do not have the responsibility or the ability to transform our child's heart. What we can do, however, is help our kids *understand* what is going on inside their hearts. But the changing and the transforming part is entirely God's gig, and He does it by His grace.

> We do not have the responsibility or the ability to transform our child's heart. But we can help them *understand* what is going on inside of it.

Our job is to treat our children the way that God, in Christ, treats us: "God is kind, but he's not soft. In kindness He takes us firmly by the hand and leads us into a radical life-change" (Romans 2:4 MSG).

I just love the visual I get when I read this verse in the Message paraphrase. Isn't it so beautiful? God isn't soft, but He is kind. He is firm, but He is also gentle. He puts His hand in ours and leads us into a transformed, God-glorifying, freedom-full way of life. It is His kindness and patience, not His wrath and fury, that turns us toward repentance and transformation. That is precisely the way I pray my children will look back on their childhood and remember me—reflecting the heart of God in how I lead them. I bet you do, too. And yet, oh friend, I am painfully aware of how often this is not the way I lead, and I know I'm not alone.

I receive countless emails through my website from women who say something very similar. One mom wrote:

> I ride a roller coaster of emotions with my kids. I feel like I do well, really well, in parenting, then bad, really bad. I'm having trouble with self-control and anger. And then the shame comes. This is not the mom I want them to remember. Sure, I'm human, but they don't deserve this. How can I handle these normal kid-parent moments with a cooler head? How can I remember all I know about grace and God during the heat of the moment? I'm not shooting for perfection, just less wounds that cut deep.

Indeed, most of us struggle with the roller coaster of emotions—the good mom moments mingling with the awful mom moments—and we're looking for tangible help to control our outbursts and anger.

4. Is There a Place for Anger in Our Discipline?

As we search the Scriptures for guidance on discipline, we find an overwhelming and undeniable theme that convicts me to the core—the danger of anger. Let's take a look at just a few of the verses that speak to this:

James 1:19–12 says, "Be quick to listen, slow to speak, and slow to become angry, for the anger of man does not produce the righteousness of God." So many of my parenting regrets are a result of me not heeding this wisdom. Indeed, I've never seen my anger produce repentance in my kids. Only shame and sadness.

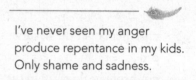

I've never seen my anger produce repentance in my kids. Only shame and sadness.

In Galatians 6:1–2, Paul writes, "Brothers and sisters, if someone is caught in a sin, you who live by the Spirit should restore that person *gently*. But watch yourselves, or you also may be tempted. Carry each other's burdens, and in this way you will fulfill the law of Christ."

In other words, if our child is caught in sin, we—who are "living by" the Holy Spirit—should correct them gently. How easy it is for us to also fall into sin in the way we correct them— be it through anger, shame, or fear tactics. A *broken together* approach is how we fulfill the law of Christ in our parenting.

In Colossians 3:21, which is actually a direct command for parents in child rearing, we are instructed, "Parents, don't come down too hard on your children or you'll crush their spirits" (MSG).

Making our kids feel bad won't make them want to be good.

It just drives them deeper into despair. Rather than coming down on them in anger or shame, we must come alongside them in grace.

> Making our kids feel bad won't make them want to be good. It just drives them into despair.

And in Ephesians 6:4, which again is a direct command to parents, we are instructed, "Fathers, do not provoke your children to anger by the way you treat them. Rather, bring them up with the discipline and instruction that comes from the Lord" (NLT).

If we twist Scripture to get our children to obey, if we hammer them over the head with the commandments of God, or if we provoke them to anger because we lash out with our own, we have not brought them up in the discipline and instruction of the Lord.

The discipline and instruction that comes from the Lord is grounded in love. Remember, while their choices may require correction and consequences, there is *no condemnation in Christ* (Romans 8:1).

Now, I am not saying that it is wrong to feel anger. I'm reminded of Ephesians 4:26 in which the apostle Paul writes, "Be angry and do not sin" (ESV). See, there is a difference in sinful anger and righteous anger, which I think is worth noting before we move on.

Righteous anger is essentially being angry about the things that make God angry. In an article about this very topic, John Bloom says that *righteous anger* is "being angered over evil that profanes God's holiness and perverts God's goodness." He goes on to say:

> Righteous anger doesn't look or feel like sinful anger because godly righteous anger is governed and directed by

love. God is righteous, but he is also love (1 John 4:8). And love is patient (1 Corinthians 13:4).

That's why God repeatedly describes himself in Scripture as "merciful and gracious, slow to anger, and abounding in steadfast love and faithfulness . . .

Being angry and not sinning requires the discernment of constant practice (Hebrews 5:14) because so much of our anger *is* rooted in our prideful, selfish sin nature. . . .

We will never be perfectly angry in this age. But we can grow in the grace of righteous anger. God means us to. It is part of being conformed to the image of Christ (Romans 8:29).[1]

Moms, to be conformed to the image of Christ and reflect His heart in our parenting, we must surrender any right we feel we have to sinful anger—to act harshly and unkindly to our kids. And we do this by first remembering God's kindness to us in Jesus Christ.

When I fail to show kindness to my kids, it's because I've forgotten how kind God has been to me in Christ.

When I fail to show kindness to my kids, it's because I've forgotten how kind God has been to me in Christ.

When I fail to show mercy, it's because I've forgotten the mercy that God has shown me in Christ.

When I fail to have patience, it's because I've forgotten how patient God has been to me.

Are we seeing how becoming a better, more grace-filled mom doesn't happen by trying harder? It happens by more deeply believing the Gospel for ourselves!

I'd like to offer two very simple but effective tools for doing this *before* we let our anger win and lose it on our kids.

1. *Don't do anything in the heat of the moment.* I used to think I had to deal with every little grievance right on the spot. But I've learned it's okay to say, "I need a time-out. I need to take this to Jesus. I'll get back to you on this, because I can't be who I need to be at this moment." Yes, Mom, you can take a time-out! And when you do, ask Jesus to help you remember your own brokenness and empower you to parent through the Cross. In doing this, we model for our kids how to *respond* rather than *react*.

2. *Pray—right there, right then.* When I find myself on the verge of yelling at my kids, you know what I try to do? Yell out to God instead. I'm not kidding. "Lord, this is an emergency! I need You and I need You now! I am angry, and I know I'm not honoring You or obeying You when I come down on my kids. Please help me right now." I might sound crazy to you and look nuts to my kids, but I'm okay looking nuts for Jesus. It seems like a better choice than going nuts on my kids. And it teaches our kids to take anything and all things to Jesus.

> I'm okay looking nuts for Jesus. It seems like a better choice than going nuts on my kids.

We're *always* teaching them something, aren't we!

5. Is It Ever Too Late to Give My Kids Grace?

Another email I received was from a mom of a tween daughter and a teenage son. She wrote:

> Grace seems scary to me. It's not how I was raised, and it's not how my husband and I have raised our kids so far. We're afraid it's too late to try it now. And we're not even sure it will work with our kids.

This email reflects many of the concerns and even fears that most of us have about this parenting with grace thing. So let's keep digging for answers . . . and hope.

I was recently with a beautiful girl in her mid-twenties who was reflecting on how the tumultuous way she was parented influenced many of the poor decisions she made.

She then went on to say, "But several months ago, my parents invited my siblings and me for dinner. And that evening, we all sat in the living room while my mom and dad apologized and asked for our forgiveness. They confessed the many mistakes they'd made and the lack of unconditional love they showed. It was one of the most powerful and healing moments in my life, and I know my siblings felt the same. We know they did the best they knew how to do, and while we all suffered from some of their mistakes, we all see how God's hand was on each of us through it all."

Her story was an important reminder that whether we are in the early stages of our parenting journey or our kids have long ago left the house and started families of their own, it is never too late to parent our kids in grace and say something like:

> This parenting thing can be hard and confusing, and I don't always know what I am doing. So I want to say I am sorry for the times I have not reflected God's heart to you and have not acted as a vessel of God's love for you. I'd give anything to go back and get less wrong and get more right.
>
> I am just beginning to understand what grace means. I've had a hard time accepting God's unconditional love for me in all of my weaknesses and failures, so it's been very hard for me to show you God's unconditional love for you in your weaknesses and failures.
>
> But I want to do it differently, and with God's help, and by God's grace, I will. Please forgive me.

It is *never, ever* too late to give our kids grace, because it is never, ever too late to give love.

It is *never, ever* too late to give our kids grace, because it is never, ever too late to give love. We don't have to be afraid to be vulnerable with our kids about this. They don't need us to be perfect and all-knowing. In fact, they already know we aren't. Our confession isn't going to be a shocking news flash for our kids. Instead, they will find great relief in our willingness to acknowledge our own imperfection and struggles. Remember, we can be broken together.

6. Is It Ever Too Early to Give My Kids Grace?

If you're balancing a one-year-old on your left hip while holding this book in your right hand, you might be asking, "How is this applicable to my parenting *now*?" Let's start by acknowledging that your main job right now is to ensure your child doesn't crawl up the stairs alone, eat from the dog's bowl, or stick her finger in an electric socket, right? I mean, really, you're focused on the basics while trying to control the chaos and make it through the fog of "littles." If you have a few clean dishes in the cabinets and everyone has at least one pair of clean underwear, you feel like a rock star, as you should! I get it.

While I totally appreciate the expression, "Big kids, big problems; little kids, little problems," I also think we absolutely cannot negate how overwhelming, exhausting, and depleting the little years can be. It does no good, anyhow, to rank levels of difficulty in motherhood, right? Each stage has its *hard*, its *holy*, and its *happy*.

If you find yourself with littles in your home, I want to give you this encouragement: There is never a better time than now to start using the "language of grace," which is essentially the language of unconditional love. Weave it into your parenting now. Love isn't for later. Love is for now. It doesn't have to compute perfectly for them now. You are practicing the language of grace and planting the seeds of grace in their hearts.

7. What Is the Language of Grace?

The language of grace is meant to help our children understand that our desire is for them to grow physically, mentally, emotionally, and spiritually. It reminds our children that what we require of them is always intended for their good and God's glory, and it is always about helping them grow into the incredible man or woman God created them to be. Most important, the language of grace ensures our children that they remain lovable even when they make unlovable choices.

> The language of grace ensures our children that they remain lovable even when they make unlovable choices.

While I am not suggesting that you speak these exact expressions to your children, this is the *mind-set* we want to have. The words you chose will be dependent on how you naturally communicate with your children and their level of maturity. But no matter their age, using the language of grace can be our mind-set.

We want our kids to know:

- I require obedience *from* you because I am *for* you.
- Your good behavior does not make you more lovable. Your misbehavior does not make you less lovable.
- Because I love you, I will discipline your disobedience, just as the Lord disciplines those He loves (Proverbs 3:12).
- I give you boundaries, and I'm consistent with those boundaries, because I want you to experience the freedom and fullness of life that Jesus purchased for you on the Cross. I will be faithful to guide you in truth.

- I understand why you struggle with _____.
  I also struggle with _____. You need
  the Holy Spirit to work in your life, and if
  you love Jesus, He *is* working in your life. You
  need a helper, a rescuer, who can help you.
- Because of what Jesus Christ did for you, there is
  absolutely no behavior, no sin, no disobedience
  that can make God stop loving you.
- When you _____, God still loves you
  and doesn't give up on you. In fact, He tells
  you to run to Him, repent, receive His mercy,
  and rely on His Spirit to obey Him.
- When you _____, God isn't mad at you. Your sin
  breaks His heart, but it doesn't break His promise to
  keep loving you.

Perhaps an even more useful exercise is comparing the language of shame to the language of grace.

8. What Is the Language of Shame?

The language of shame equates what we do with the core of who we are. It makes hurtful and blanket statements. It relies on fear and anger to produce change in our children's hearts. It forgets the Cross.

- After all I've done for you, you still go and _____.
- How many times do I have to tell you to _____.
- You never_____.
- You always_____.
- How could you_____.
- Who does something like _____.
- If only you were more _____.
- You should be ashamed of yourself for _____.
- Why can't you just _____.
- God is going to get sick of you asking Him for forgiveness for _____.
- How can you call yourself a Christian, when you _____.

There's a radical difference between words of grace and words of shame, right?

While our children may not understand everything we're saying, we are practicing a language (whether it be grace or shame) that will have a profound impact on our relationship with them and on their relationship with God.

And on the days when we *fail* to respond with grace—like

when we throw a temper tantrum that rivals theirs, or we throw shame at their failure, or we rely on empty threats and fear tactics to change their behavior—we can remember the grace that is available to us in that very moment, lavishly poured out on us when we fail. We can welcome His grace, be led to repentance, seek our child's forgiveness, and surrender—again—to the Holy Spirit's transforming power in our own heart.

9. What If My Kids Take Advantage of Grace?

I think we're sometimes afraid that grace will "backfire" in the lives of our kids. That our kids will abuse it and misuse it.

But if you've personally tasted grace, you know its sweetness. You know that grace is what *inspires* us—out of devotion and gratitude— to chase hard after God because we can barely believe the extent to which He went to rescue us.

> Grace inspires us to chase hard after God because you can barely believe the extent He went to chase hard after us, in Jesus.

There's only one thing that has the power to help us overcome sin, and Paul tells us what that is in a letter he wrote to Titus: "For the grace of God . . . teaches us to say 'No' to ungodliness and worldly passions, and to live self-controlled, upright, and godly lives in the present age" (2:11–12, NIV).

Grace is portrayed as our "teacher" here, and what it *teaches* us is to say "no to ungodliness." Grace inspires us to say *no* to sin and *yes* to godliness!

It is love and gratitude for Christ that inspires obedience to Christ. Not law, but *love*. The law shows us how to live. Grace, by the power of the Holy Spirit, inspires us to action. We need to know this! God's love is not *dependent* on how well we obey the law. His love does, however, make us *desire* to obey the law.

In light of these truths, grace is no longer scary. In fact, it becomes the very thing to which we cling and hang our hopes in our parenting.

Our kids may very well take advantage of grace in the here and now. It's probably safe to say we do too. It's part of that whole being human thing!

> God's love is not *dependent* on how well we obey the law. His love does, however, make us *desire* to obey the law.

10. When Will We See the Fruit of Grace?

Finally, we want to know when we will see grace produce fruit in the lives of our kids. And the truthful answer is probably not today. And let's just be honest about how we feel about that. We don't like it. Or maybe I should just speak for myself. *I* don't like it. I want to see my hard work paying off now. Or at least quickly. I want to see fruit right away because it makes my life easier. That whole dying-to-self thing in parenting is something God is still faithfully working out in me. But more important, I want to see the fruit of grace right away because I want my kids to live in the fullness and abundance of life that Jesus left heaven to give them (John 10:10). But, unfortunately, we have no control over how and when grace grips our children's hearts. In fact, the fruit of grace is almost always in the future. Just because we give our kids grace does not mean grace will penetrate their hearts on our time line and make them want to hang on to Jesus because He hung on a cross for them.

Scripture doesn't say, "He who began a good work in you will finish it by Friday." It says, "Being confident of this, that He who began a good work in you will carry it on to completion until the day of Christ Jesus" (Philippians 1:6). God does not work on our time line. And if we knew everything He knows, I think we'd be pretty thankful about that.

> Scripture doesn't say, "He who began a good work in you will finish it by Friday."

What we know for certain is that law-laden parenting is not what Scripture tells us will inspire or enable the human heart to devotion or obedience to God. It'll change behavior. But it won't change hearts. And ultimately, it can drive our kids away from their faith because they will give up on ever being good enough to keep God happy.

But intentional, grace-based, Gospel-centered parenting draws kids into the loving arms of their heavenly Father, who transforms rebellious hearts. Let's now take a closer look at how that transformation happens.

P.S.: As I'm sure you've guessed by now, my answer to Brennan's question, which I shared with you at the beginning of this chapter, was "I did give you grace, buddy. I was firm but kind. And I disciplined you out of love. *That* is grace."

CHAPTER 18

Transforming Grace

Nurturing Gratitude for God's
Grace in Our Children's Hearts

Perhaps you've heard of a "family mission statement"? Perhaps you have one?

Before my eldest was born, I was given the wonderful advice to choose a Bible verse that would serve as our "family mission statement"—a verse that would reflect what is most important to us and would guide us in our decision-making as a family.

I loved the idea, and didn't have to think long about which verse to choose.

I had a very clear picture of what I wanted to create—a home with God-loving and God-obeying kids. The Greatest Commandment was my obvious and immediate choice.

Scripture says,

Hearing that Jesus had silenced the Sadducees,
the Pharisees got together. One of them, an expert
in the law, tested him with this question:
"Teacher, which is the greatest commandment in the
Law?" Jesus replied: " 'Love the Lord your God with
all your heart and with all your soul and with all your
mind.' This is the first and greatest commandment. And
the second is like it: 'Love your neighbor as yourself.' "
(Matthew 22:34–39 NIV)

As you've discovered by now, my previous focus had always been on earning acceptance *from* God through my good behavior *for* God; so naturally, I was going to parent my young children using this principle. My starting place was that they should love God by obeying His rules and having good behavior to keep Him happy.

So I made a long list of "House Rules for Godly Growth"—which was essentially a list of Christ-like virtues—posted it on our refrigerator, and got busy trying to produce the fruit of the Spirit in my kids' lives. Along with each virtue, I listed a Bible verse or two, so I could refer to God's Word when instructing them.

What I didn't understand back in those law-laden days is that *knowledge* of God's law does not beget the *ability* or *desire* to obey God's law, as we just discussed in the previous chapter. I didn't get that Bible verses posted on bulletin boards wouldn't produce a love for God's Word in my children's hearts.

Am I saying that we should not store the Word of God in the hearts of our kids and teach them to follow Him with all their heart and soul and mind? Of course not. Giving our kids God's

Word—every day—is, in fact, one of the greatest gifts we can give them.

But even if we have "House Rules for Godly Growth" and Bible verses on display in our homes, we must understand this: Only as our children come to know that Jesus *already* fulfilled the law on our behalf will they be enlivened to obey the greatest commandment.

In fact, a Barna Group study revealed that the number one challenge to people growing spiritually is that most people equate spiritual maturity with trying hard to follow the rules in the Bible.[1] This finding shouldn't surprise us; the apostle Paul warned us of this very thing in the book of Galatians when he wrote:

> Rule-keeping does not naturally evolve into living by faith, but only perpetuates itself in more and more rule-keeping, a fact observed in Scripture: "The one who does these things [rule-keeping] continues to live by them." Christ redeemed us from that self-defeating, cursed life by absorbing it completely into himself (Galatians 3:12–14 MSG).

Christ has redeemed our children from trying hard to follow the rules to keep God pleased. Now they are free to chase hard after Him! This is the Good News that breeds gratitude in their hearts and the beautiful message we must make central in our homes!

> Christ has redeemed our children from trying hard to follow the rules to keep God pleased.

A Beautiful Picture of Transforming Grace

The transforming power of grace is beautifully demonstrated in countless stories in the Bible, but one of my favorites is found in the gospel of Luke 7:36–48.

> *One of the Pharisees asked [Jesus] over for a meal. He went to the Pharisee's house and sat down at the dinner table. Just then a woman of the village, the town harlot, having learned that Jesus was a guest in the home of the Pharisee, came with a bottle of very expensive perfume and stood at his feet, weeping, raining tears on his feet. Letting down her hair, she dried his feet, kissed them, and anointed them with the perfume. When the Pharisee who had invited him saw this, he said to himself, "If this man was the prophet I thought he was, he would have known what kind of woman this is who is falling all over him."*
>
> *Jesus said to him, "Simon, I have something to tell you."*
>
> *"Oh? Tell me."*
>
> *"Two men were in debt to a banker. One owed five hundred silver pieces, the other fifty. Neither of them could pay up, and so the banker canceled both debts. Which of the two would be more grateful?"*
>
> *Simon answered, "I suppose the one who was forgiven the most."*
>
> *"That's right," said Jesus. Then turning to the woman, but speaking to Simon, he said, "Do you see this woman? I came to your home; you provided no water for my feet, but she rained tears on my feet and dried them with her hair. You gave me no greeting, but from the time I arrived, she hasn't quit*

kissing my feet. You provided nothing for freshening up, but she has soothed my feet with perfume. Impressive, isn't it? "She was forgiven many, many sins, and so she is very, very grateful. If the forgiveness is minimal, the gratitude is minimal."
(MSG)

Isn't that a beautiful story! This woman was forgiven much, so she loved much. It was her *gratitude* for the forgiveness she knew she needed, and that she received, that cracked her open to repentance—that place where grace can do its transforming work. Likewise, when we recognize our many, many sins that Jesus daily forgives, we become very, very grateful for His daily grace. A grace that doesn't make us want to keep on sinning, but a grace that makes us want to fall at His feet in worship.

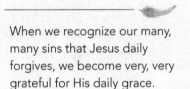

> When we recognize our many, many sins that Jesus daily forgives, we become very, very grateful for His daily grace.

So now let's apply this passage to our parenting and identify three practical things we can do to nurture this kind of gratitude in our kids' hearts on a daily basis.

Remember, Rely, and Recognize

We can help our kids:

1. *Remember* what Jesus has already done for us.
2. *Rely* on the power He gives us to live in obedience.
3. *Recognize* His faithfulness to grow us.

1. Remember What Jesus Has Already Done for Us

Before asking our children to *respond as Jesus would*, let's first help them *remember what Jesus has already done.*

> Before asking our children to *respond as Jesus would,* let's first help them *remember what Jesus has already done.*

Now, if you're anything like me, reminding your children of what Jesus has done wouldn't necessarily be your natural response. Instead, your first instinct might be to point out what your children did wrong and then throw in a Bible verse, for good measure, to show them how to do it right. (And sometimes that's all we can do with the time or bandwidth we've got, and that's okay, too!)

So let's take a look at a few examples of how we can help our children *first* remember what Jesus has already done, and *then* instruct them how to respond as He would.

When our children are being unkind to one another, we can:

- *First,* take a moment to remember how Jesus demonstrated the ultimate act of kindness in laying down His life for us while we were still sinners (Romans 5:8). To bring home Jesus' love for sinners, we can point our children to stories such as the one we find in Luke 19, where Jesus showed kindness to even the most unkind people like Zacchaeus.
- *Then* we can turn to Scripture that instructs us in kindness, such as Colossians 3:12, "Clothe

yourselves with compassion, kindness,
humility, gentleness, and patience" (NIV).

*When our children don't want to seek forgiveness from one
another or grant forgiveness to one another,* we can:

- *First,* take a moment to remember that God has
  already forgiven every sin we have ever or will ever
  commit because of what Jesus did for us on the Cross
  (Psalm 103:8–13).
    To bring home the forgiveness of Christ, we can
    point them to stories like the one we find in John
    21:15–25, where Jesus forgave even Peter—who
    disowned and betrayed him before his death.
- *Then* we can turn to Scripture that instructs us in
  forgiveness, such as Ephesians 4:32, "Be kind and
  compassionate to one another, forgiving each other,
  just as in Christ God forgave you" (NIV).

*When our children don't want to obey us or submit to our
authority,* we can:

- *First,* take a moment to remember how Jesus humbly
  submitted to His Father and obeyed Him, even unto
  death (Luke 22:39–44).
- *Then* we can turn to Scripture that instructs our
  children in obeying us and, ultimately God, such as
  Ephesians 6:1, "Obey your parents in the Lord, for
  this is right" (NIV).

2. Rely on the Power He Gives Us to Live in Obedience

As we teach our children to remember Jesus, we can also teach them to *rely* on Jesus. As I often remind my boys when they are struggling with a particular sin or weakness: "Don't try to overcome this in your own power. Rely on the power of Christ that is within you, because 'the One who lives in you is stronger than the one who is in the world' " (1 John 4:4 NLT).

For example, in John 15:4–5, Jesus says, "Abide in me, and I in you. As the branch cannot bear fruit by itself, unless it abides in the vine, neither can you, unless you abide in me. I am the vine; you are the branches. Whoever abides in me and I in him, he it is that bears much fruit, for apart from me you can do nothing" (ESV).

> We grow in holiness to the degree that we allow Jesus to take up residence in our hearts.

What Jesus is teaching us in this passage is this: we grow in holiness to the degree that we allow Jesus to take up residence in our hearts.

Apart from Him, we can do no good thing. He doesn't say we can do *some* good without him. He says very plainly, "You can't produce the fruit of the Spirit by yourself."

It's the indwelling of the Holy Spirit that produces the fruit of the Spirit—the "love, joy, peace, forbearance, kindness, goodness, faithfulness, gentleness, and self-control—in our children's lives (Galatians 5:22–23 NIV). We can't do this on our own, and neither can our kids.

When Paul writes in Romans 8:37, "In all things we are more than conquerors through Him who loved us," there is a reason he used the word *through* and that he didn't say *for*. God hasn't called us to be conquerors *for* Him. We are only conquerors *through* Him.

God hasn't called us to be conquerors *for* Him. We are only conquerors *through* Him.

Does the story of David and Goliath come to mind? It's the story in the Old Testament where God chose David—the youngest and weakest of all his brothers—to defeat the giant, Goliath, because David's victory would point, not to man's strength, but to God's strength alone. God showed off his strength in David's weakness. Even more important, this story sets the stage for another unlikely and greater hero (Jesus), who would soon come to defeat even bigger giants—sin and death.

How often do I try to live in the *likeness* of Christ without relying on the *power* of Christ? Too often! But reminding my boys reminds me!

Apart from living in union with and utter dependence on God, we can do no good thing. We might be productive, but we won't be fruitful—and there is a profound difference in the two. God produces the fruit, for the glory and praise of His grace. Have no doubt: part of God's purpose for us is to produce character in us—character that will point others to the nature of God. And this character is produced in us only when we *rely* on Him.

3. Recognize His Faithfulness to Grow Us

And then finally, we can help our children recognize Jesus' work in their lives. I all too easily get stuck in a pattern of *instructing* and *correcting*, when I need to also be actively *looking for*, *acknowledging*, and *affirming* the fruit of God's grace in their lives. It's amazing how the countenance of my children changes when I notice—acknowledge—the fruit of the Spirit in their lives. If we see something, we should say something. And the more specific we can be, the better.

For example, I have a son who's very hard on himself. Therefore, he can be hard on those around him. This reality was most often on display during sporting events when his teammates would make mistakes.

Recognizing this struggle in his life, my son began praying that God would help him build others up and empower him to be a friend who speaks words of life and encouragement when his friends fail or struggle. It didn't take long to notice a difference in my son's demeanor on the field. After his games, it brought me so much joy to say to my son, "I noticed how you built up your teammates today, and I can't tell you how much it thrills me to see God answer that prayer and do His good work in your life."

I also have a son who struggles with his temper. I can assure you, he inherited that from me. At night when we are all snuggled into our beds, he will often pray that God would help him control his temper and in his own words, "not get so angry." It's been a privilege to watch God slowly but surely answer that prayer in my son's life. I love being able to say, "I know that you just got really angry at your brother, and I want you to know how happy it made me to see you chose self-control in your response." Of course, there are and will continue to be circumstances in which he, like me, still loses his cool. He's human. But I love seizing any opportunity I can to show him how relying on the power of Christ within him empowered him to honor God in his response.

Take a moment and ask yourself, "Where do I see God working in the lives of my kids, and how can I encourage them to see God's faithfulness to them?" Praise that recognizes the fruit of their salvation and points our kids back to God's power and grace at work in their lives is *always* a good thing. It reminds them that it's Christ work to save *and* it's Christ's work to sanctify.

If we can keep *remember*, *rely*, and *recognize* in the forefront of our minds, we will be set free from the pressure to control our children's behavior and transform their hearts. How freeing it is to know that as we seek to make the Gospel central in our homes, it's the Holy Spirit's work *alone* to lead them in heartfelt trust and obedience.

> How freeing it is to know that as we seek to make the Gospel central in our homes, it's the Holy Spirit's work *alone* to lead them in heartfelt trust and obedience.

In Closing

You're a Mom Set Free!

So, my friend, I can barely believe we are wrapping up our time together. I am so very grateful that, amidst your full life and chaotic days, you have given yourself the gift of diving deeper into God's grace.

But there is one last piece of encouragement I want to give you. We've just spent several chapters looking at how we can make the Gospel central in our homes. We've discovered how, as we remember who we are in Christ and the grace that has us covered as parents, we are inspired and empowered to be a vessel of that grace to our kids. And we are ready to see grace transform our hearts and homes.

But! In closing, I want to make sure our shoulders aren't again heavy with burdens we aren't meant to carry. I want to ensure we haven't picked up things we've been freed to lay down. And to do so, I want to share with you a recent conversation I had with a good friend.

I was wrestling with how to give my kids grace in a difficult situation, so I gave my friend Jessica Thompson a call. Jessica is the co-author of the incredible book, *Give Them Grace*, and though we are close in age, she has very much been a mentor to me through her writing and personal advice. The way she shares the Good News speaks directly to my heart.

Well, after we spent about thirty minutes talking through my questions and were preparing to hang up the phone, I could tell Jessica felt my lingering angst. Though I wasn't feeling the pressure to be a perfect mom who was raising perfect kids, I was still feeling the pressure to give grace "perfectly" to my kids.

So before we hung up, Jessica gave me one last piece of advice, and it was some of the most freeing advice I've ever been given.

"Jeannie," she gently said, "the *way* you give your kids the Gospel isn't going to determine whether they accept it or not. It's not all on you."

Friend, did you see how she framed the significance of my role in light of God's sovereignty?

In other words, yes, absolutely make every effort to make the Gospel central in your home and give your kids grace. But please (please!) don't carry the pressure of thinking that if you always give it to them the "right" way, they will come to love Jesus more, and if you always give it to them the "wrong" way, they will not come to love Jesus at all. God is good at using our weakness to show His power.

So, my dear fellow mom, will you say it with me just one more time:

I play an important role in my kids' lives, but I am not God.
I can trust God with the children He has entrusted to me.
My job isn't to be the perfection of Christ, it's to point my
*   children to Christ—the only One who has never and will*
*   never let them down.*

*God's grace is magnified in my weakness, and I am free from
the pressure to get it all right.
I can rely on the power of Christ in me.
I am a mom set free.*

With those extraordinary truths in mind, I'd love to return
to the same question I proposed earlier in our journey together.
Knowing what we know now, I ask again: *How would your life—
and your parenting—look different if you really believed and
lived from the truth that God can't stop loving you? Just as you
are, not as you wish you were.*

- What burdens can you now lay down at the Cross . . .
  because you believe He is *for* you and *can be trusted
  with your life?*
- What shame can you finally shed . . . because you
  believe there has *never been a moment of time* or even
  a minute of your life *that His heart has not belonged
  to you?*
- From what striving can you cease . . . because you
  believe Jesus has already been "good enough" for
  you and that He will *never abandon you?*
- What sin is no longer your boss . . . because you
  believe you are a new creation in Christ and you desire
  to live out of *that* identity?

See, Jesus so simply and beautifully said, "And you will know
the truth and the truth will set you free" (John 8:32 NLT). And so
I am praying, with all my heart, that the truth has set you *wildly*
free to live in the fullness of His grace!

And to help you do that (because the enemy is eager to ensure you don't!) I'd love to give you a little something. It's a collection of Bible verses that has been instrumental in my own journey of remembering God's grace and sovereignty. We have read most of these verses throughout our journey together, but I thought it might be helpful to have them collected into one place for easy reference.

I hope you will run back to these passages over and over again when the voice of that merciless critic comes knocking. I hope this collection will help you believe that what God says about you is true and will empower you to rest in all He's done for you. You'll find these verses in the following chapter.

And finally, I want you to know I am praying for you. As you hold this book in your hands, I am praying that God will surround you with other brave women who want to live authentic lives anchored in the Good News of God's wild grace. And I am praying that you will inspire other moms to get real with each other—to not just talk about their successes but also share their shortcomings, sins, and sorrows. Not to celebrate our sin, of course, but to have a safe place to find healing and forgiveness, to grow in grace, and to discover more of what it means to live and parent in the freedom of God's unwavering love.

So before we close, I'd also love to pray *with* you, asking God to seal in our hearts all that He has shown us through these pages. Can we go to God together in prayer now?

Heavenly Father...
You are beautiful.
You are faithful and kind and compassionate and good.

You are everything we need and everything our hearts long for.

You are sovereign and full of grace.

So we boldly come before you now and ask that You would help us . . .

Believe we are Your beloved and help us overcome our disbelief.

Believe what You say over what we see.

Live by faith, not by sight.

Remember Your faithfulness in the past as we face the uncertainty of the future.

Desire the assurance of Your presence more than answers to our questions.

Lay down all that You have not asked us to carry so that we can thrive in what You have.

Trust Your sovereignty over our significance in the lives of our children.

Make the Good News of Jesus—not the good behavior of our children—the foundation on which we build.

Stop trying so hard and start enjoying the children You have entrusted to us.

Rely on the Holy Spirit to produce the fruit of the Spirit in their lives.

Be a reflection of Your heart and a vessel of Your love.

Parent with wonder over worry, faith over fear, connection over control, joy over anger, humility over pride, and love over shame.

And finally, help us . . .

Impress upon our children a love for You that is anchored in Your love for them.

Lord, more than anything else, we want to nurture in them a sincere longing to know You, trust You, follow You, serve You, and love You—the only One who has always been and will always be their Perfect Parent and Sovereign Savior.

We love you. We thank you. We praise and adore you.

In your beautiful and wonderful and powerful name we pray, Amen.

Breathe in grace, dear mom. You are covered. You are *free*.

Bible Verses

To Help You *Breathe in Grace*

When you need to be reminded how very much God loves you (and is going to keep on loving you!):

> *Absolutely nothing can get between us and God's love because of the way that Jesus our Master has embraced us.*
> —Romans 8:39 MSG

> *God did not keep His own Son for*
> *Himself but gave Him for us all.*
> *Then with His Son, will He not give us all things?*
> —Romans 8:32 NLV

> *Immense in mercy and with an incredible love, he embraced us.*
> *He took our sin-dead lives and made us alive in Christ.*
> *He did all this on his own, with no help from us!*
> *Then he picked us up and set us down in highest*
> *heaven in company with Jesus, our Messiah.*
> —Ephesians 2:4–5 MSG

So now there is no condemnation for those
who belong to Christ Jesus.
—Romans 8:1 NLT

The Lord is compassionate and gracious,
slow to anger, abounding in love.
He will not always accuse, nor will he harbor his anger forever;
He does not treat us as our sins deserve or
repay us according to our iniquities.
For as high as the heavens are above the earth,
so great is his love for those who fear him;
as far as the east is from the west, so far has he
removed our transgressions from us.
—Psalm 103:8–12 NIV

But he was pierced for our rebellion, crushed for our sins.
He was beaten so we could be whole. He
was whipped so we could be healed.
All of us, like sheep, have strayed away.
We have left God's paths to follow our own.
Yet the Lord laid on him the sins of us all.
—Isaiah 53:5–6 NLT

This is how we know what love is: Jesus
Christ laid down his life for us.
—1 John 3:16 NIV

I pray that Christ may live in your hearts by faith.
I pray that you will be filled with love.

*I pray that you will be able to understand how wide and
how long and how high and how deep His love is.
I pray that you will know the love of Christ.
His love goes beyond anything we can understand.
I pray that you will be filled with God Himself.*
—Ephesians 3:17–19 NLV

*God told them, "I've never quit loving you and never will.
Expect love, love, and more love!"*
—Jeremiah 31:3–6 MSG

*W*hen you're weak, worried, exhausted, and burned out:

*And he knows everything, inside and out.
He energizes those who get tired, gives
fresh strength to dropouts.
For even young people tire and drop out, young
folk in their prime stumble and fall.
But those who wait upon God get fresh strength.
They spread their wings and soar like eagles,
They run and don't get tired, they walk and don't lag behind.*
—Isaiah 40: 27–31 MSG

*Are you tired? Worn out? Burned out on religion?
Come to me. Get away with me and you'll recover your life.
I'll show you how to take a real rest.
Walk with me and work with me—watch how I do it.*

235

Learn the unforced rhythms of grace.
I won't lay anything heavy or ill-fitting on you.
Keep company with me and you'll learn to live freely and lightly.
—Matthew 11:28–30 MSG

The Lord himself will fight for you. Just stay calm.
—Exodus 14:14 NLT

Now that we know what we have—
Jesus, this great High Priest with ready access to God—
let's not let it slip through our fingers.
We don't have a priest who is out of touch with our reality.
He's been through weakness and testing, experienced it all—
all but the sin. So let's walk right up to him
and get what he is so ready to give.
Take the mercy, accept the help.
—Hebrews 4:15–16 MSG

This is what the Sovereign Lord, the Holy One of Israel, says:
In repentance and rest is your salvation, in quietness and
trust is your strength, but you would have none of it.
—Isaiah 30:15 NIV

Each time he said, "My grace is all you need.
My power works best in weakness."
So now I am glad to boast about my weaknesses, so
that the power of Christ can work through me.
—2 Corinthians 12:9 NLT

Let the Holy Spirit guide your lives.
Then you won't be doing what your sinful nature craves.
The sinful nature wants to do evil,
which is just the opposite of what the Spirit wants.
And the Spirit gives us desires that are
the opposite of what the sinful nature desires.
These two forces are constantly fighting each other,
so you are not free to carry out your good intentions.
—Galatians 5:16–17 NLT

Abide in me, and I in you.
As the branch cannot bear fruit by itself,
unless it abides in the vine,
neither can you, unless you abide in me.
I am the vine; you are the branches.
Whoever abides in me and I in him, he it is that bears
much fruit, for apart from me you can do nothing.
—John 15:4–5 ESV

Don't worry about anything; instead, pray about everything.
Tell God what you need, and thank him for all he has done.
Then you will experience God's peace, which
exceeds anything we can understand.
His peace will guard your hearts and minds
as you live in Christ Jesus.
—Philippians 4:6–7 NLT

The One Who called you is faithful
and will do what He promised.
—1 Thessalonians 5:24 NLV

*W*hen you're trying to be good enough for God:

Everything that goes into a life of pleasing God
has been miraculously given to us by getting to know,
personally and intimately, the One who invited us to God.
The best invitation we ever received!
—2 Peter 1:3–4 MSG

Even before he made the world, God loved us and chose
us in Christ to be holy and without fault in his eyes.
God decided in advance to adopt us into his own family
by bringing us to himself through Jesus Christ.
This is what he wanted to do, and it gave him great pleasure.
—Ephesians 1:4–5 NLT

God made him who had no sin to be sin for us, so that
in him we might become the righteousness of God.
—2 Corinthians 5:21 NIV

When God our Savior revealed his kindness and
love, he saved us, not because of the righteous
things we had done, but because of his mercy.
He washed away our sins, giving us a new birth
and new life through the Holy Spirit.
—Titus 3:4–5 NLT

I've tried everything and nothing helps.
I'm at the end of my rope.
Is there no one who can do anything for me?
Isn't that the real question?
The answer, thank God, is that Jesus Christ can and does.
He acted to set things right in this life of contradictions
where I want to serve God with all my heart and mind,
but am pulled by the influence of sin to
do something totally different.
—Romans 7:24–25 MSG

For it is by grace you have been saved, through faith—
and this is not from yourselves, it is the gift of God—
not by works, so that no one can boast.
—Ephesians 2:8–9 NIV

When we were utterly helpless,
Christ came at just the right time and died for us sinners.
Now, most people would not be willing
to die for an upright person,
though someone might perhaps be willing to
die for a person who is especially good.
But God showed his great love for us by sending
Christ to die for us while we were still sinners.
—Romans 5:6–8 NLT

Going through the motions doesn't please you,
a flawless performance is nothing to you.
I learned God-worship when my pride was shattered.

Heart-shattered lives ready for love don't
for a moment escape God's notice.
—Psalm 51:16–17 MSG

For no one can ever be made right with God
by doing what the law commands.
The law simply shows us how sinful we are.
But now God has shown us a way to be made right with
him without keeping the requirements of the law,
as was promised in the writings of Moses
and the prophets long ago.
We are made right with God by placing our faith in Jesus Christ.
And this is true for everyone who believes,
no matter who we are. For everyone has sinned;
we all fall short of God's glorious standard.
Yet God freely and graciously declares that we are righteous.
He did this through Christ Jesus when he
freed us from the penalty for our sins.
—Romans 3:20–24 NLT

Because of his great love for us, God, who is rich in mercy,
made us alive with Christ even when we
were dead in transgressions—
it is by grace you have been saved.
—Ephesians 2:4–5 NIV

We know very well that we are not set right with God by
rule-keeping but only through personal faith in Jesus Christ.
How do we know?

*We tried it—and we had the best system
of rules the world has ever seen!
Convinced that no human being can please God
by self-improvement, we believed in Jesus as the
Messiah so that we might be set right before God by
trusting in the Messiah, not by trying to be good.*
—Galatians 2:15–16 MSG

*W*hen you need to remember God's sovereignty:

*And we know that God causes everything to work
together for the good of those who love God and
are called according to his purpose for them.*
—Romans 8:28 NLT

*At the right time he will bring everything
together under the authority of Christ—
everything in heaven and on earth.
Furthermore, because we are united with Christ,
we have received an inheritance from God,
for he chose us in advance, and he makes
everything work out according to his plan.*
—Ephesians 1:10–11 NLT

*Jesus replied, "Your mistake is that you don't know the
Scriptures, and you don't know the power of God."*
—Matthew 22:29 NLT

*For the Lord God says, "I am the First and the Last,
the beginning and the end of all things.*

I am the All-powerful One Who was
and Who is and Who is to come."
—Revelation 1:8 NLV

You saw me before I was born.
Every day of my life was recorded in your book.
Every moment was laid out.
—Psalm 139:16 NLT

We can make our plans,
but the Lord determines our steps.
—Proverbs 16:9 NLT

For my thoughts are not your thoughts,
neither are your ways my ways, declares the Lord.
For as the heavens are higher than the earth,
so are my ways higher than your ways,
and my thoughts than your thoughts.
—Isaiah 55:8–9 ESV

I know what I'm doing. I have it all planned out—
plans to take care of you, not abandon you,
plans to give you the future you hope for.
—Jeremiah 29:11 MSG

It won't be long before this generous God
who has great plans for us in Christ—
eternal and glorious plans they are!—
will have you put together and on your feet for good.
He gets the last word; yes, he does!
—1 Peter 5:10–11 MSG

Be still and know that I am God.
—Psalm 46:10 NIV

As for God, His way is perfect: The Lord's word is flawless;
He shields all who take refuge in Him.
—Psalm 18:30 NIV

God's Spirit is right alongside helping us along.
If we don't know how or what to pray, it doesn't matter.
He does our praying in and for us, making prayer
out of our wordless sighs, our aching groans.
He knows us far better than we know ourselves,
knows our pregnant condition, and keeps us present before God.
That's why we can be so sure that every detail in our
lives of love for God is worked into something good.
—Romans 8:26–28 MSG

Furthermore, because we are united with Christ, we have
received an inheritance from God, for he chose us in advance,
and he makes everything work out according to his plan.
—Ephesians 1:11 NLT

When you're heartbroken and hopeless:

If your heart is broken, you'll find God right there;
if you're kicked in the gut, he'll help you catch your breath.
—Psalm 34:18 MSG

If you don't know what you're doing, pray to the Father.
He loves to help.
—James 1:5 MSG

God can do anything, you know—
far more than you could ever imagine or guess
or request in your wildest dreams!
He does it not by pushing us around but by working
within us, his Spirit deeply and gently within us.
—Ephesians 3:20–21a MSG

I have told you all this so that you may have peace in me.
Here on earth you will have many trials and sorrows.
But take heart, because I have overcome the world.
—John 16:33 NLT

We can rejoice, too, when we run into problems and trials,
for we know that they help us develop endurance.
And endurance develops strength of character,
and character strengthens our confident hope of salvation.
And this hope will not lead to disappointment.
For we know how dearly God loves us,
because he has given us the Holy Spirit
to fill our hearts with his love.
—Romans 5:3–5 NLT

The Spirit himself testifies with our spirit
that we are God's children.
Now if we are children, then we are heirs—
heirs of God and co-heirs with Christ,
if indeed we share in his sufferings in order
that we may also share in his glory.
I consider that our present sufferings are not worth
comparing with the glory that will be revealed in us.
—Romans 8:16–18 NIV

Yet hope returns when I remember this one thing:
The Lord's unfailing love and mercy still continue,
fresh as the morning, as sure as the sunrise.
The Lord is all I have, and so in him I put my hope.
—Lamentations 3:21–24 GNT

Being confident of this, that He who began a good work in you
will carry it on to completion until the day of Christ Jesus.
—Philippians 1:6 NIV

He will cover you with his feathers.
He will shelter you with his wings.
His faithful promises are your armor and protection.
—Psalm 91:4 NLT

In the morning, Lord, you hear my voice;
in the morning I lay my requests before you
and wait expectantly.
—Psalm 5:3 NIV

Give all your worries to Him
because He cares for you.
—1 Peter 5:7 NLV

Out of my distress I called on the Lord;
the Lord answered me and set me free.
The Lord is on my side; I will not fear.
What can man do to me?
—Psalm 118:5–6 ESV

*W*hen you need to remember who you are in Christ:

This is my Son [or daughter],
chosen and marked by my love, delight of my life.
—Matthew 3:17 MSG

For we are God's masterpiece.
He has created us anew in Christ Jesus,
so we can do the good things he planned for us long ago.
—Ephesians 2:10 NLT

We demolish arguments and every pretension
that sets itself up against the knowledge of God,
and we take captive every thought
to make it obedient to Christ.
—2 Corinthians 10:5 NIV

But now the Lord Who made you, O Jacob,
and He Who made you, O Israel, says: Do not be afraid.
For I have bought you and made you free.
I have called you by name. You are Mine!
When you pass through the waters, I will be with you.
When you pass through the rivers, they will not flow over you.
When you walk through the fire, you will not be burned.
The fire will not destroy you.
For I am the Lord your God,
the Holy One of Israel, Who saves you.
I have given Egypt as pay for your life,
and have traded Cush and Seba for you.

You are of great worth in My eyes.
You are honored and I love you.
—Isaiah 43:1–4 NLV

Dear friends, we are God's children now.
But it has not yet been shown to us what we are going to be.
We know that when He comes again,
we will be like Him because we will see Him as He is.
—1 John 3:2 NLV

For now we see only a reflection as in a mirror;
then we shall see face to face.
Now I know in part;
then I shall know fully, even as I am fully known.
—1 Corinthians 13:12 NIV

See what great love the Father has lavished on us,
that we should be called children of God!
And that is what we are!
—1 John 3:1a NIV

But to all who believed him and accepted him,
he gave the right to become children of God.
They are reborn—not with a physical birth resulting from
human passion or plan, but a birth that comes from God.
—John 1:12–13 NLT

I'll call nobodies and make them somebodies;
I'll call the unloved and make them beloved.
In the place where they yelled out, "You're nobody!"
they're calling you "God's living children."
—Romans 9:25 MSG

When you need to remember what makes you free:

What actually took place is this:
I tried keeping rules and working my head
off to please God, and it didn't work.
So I quit being a "law man" so that I could be God's man.
Christ's life showed me how, and enabled me to do it.
I identified myself completely with him.
Indeed, I have been crucified with Christ.
My ego is no longer central.
It is no longer important that I appear righteous
before you or have your good opinion,
and I am no longer driven to impress God.
Christ lives in me.
The life you see me living is not "mine," but
it is lived by faith in the Son of God,
who loved me and gave himself for me.
I am not going to go back on that.
Is it not clear to you that to go back to that old rule-keeping,
peer-pleasing religion would be an abandonment
of everything personal and free in my relationship with God?
I refuse to do that, to repudiate God's grace.
If a living relationship with God could come by rule-keeping,
then Christ died unnecessarily.
—Galatians 2:19–21 MSG

*W*hen you need to remember what you've been set free for:

It is for freedom that Christ has set us free.
Stand firm, then, and do not let yourselves be
burdened again by a yoke of slavery.
—Galatians 5:1 NIV

It is absolutely clear that God has called you to a free life.
Just make sure that you don't use this freedom as an excuse
to do whatever you want to do and destroy your freedom.
Rather, use your freedom to serve one another
in love; that's how freedom grows.
For everything we know about God's Word
is summed up in a single sentence:
Love others as you love yourself.
That's an act of true freedom.
—Galatians 5:13–14 MSG

A new command I give you: Love one another.
As I have loved you, so you must love one another.
By this everyone will know that you are my
disciples, if you love one another.
—John 13:34–35 NIV

For the grace of God has appeared,
bringing salvation for all people,
training us to renounce ungodliness and worldly passions,
and to live self-controlled, upright,
and godly lives in the present age.
—Titus 2:11–12 ESV

"Love the Lord your God with all your heart and
with all your soul and with all your mind."
This is the first and greatest commandment.
And the second is like it:
"Love your neighbor as yourself."
—Matthew 22:37–39 NIV

Then the way you live will always honor and please the Lord,
and your lives will produce every kind of good fruit.
All the while, you will grow as you learn
to know God better and better.
—Colossians 1:10 NLT

But whoever looks intently into the perfect law
that gives freedom, and continues in it—
not forgetting what they have heard, but doing it—
they will be blessed in what they do.
—James 1:25 NIV

*W*hen you need to remember that God's not mad at you:

Now that we are set right with God by
means of this sacrificial death,
the consummate blood sacrifice, there is no longer a
question of being at odds with God in any way.
If, when we were at our worst, we were put on friendly
terms with God by the sacrificial death of his Son,
now that we're at our best, just think of how our lives will
expand and deepen by means of his resurrection life!
Now that we have actually received this
amazing friendship with God,

we are no longer content to simply say it in plodding prose.
We sing and shout our praises to God
through Jesus, the Messiah!
—Romans 5:9–11 MSG

But sin didn't, and doesn't, have a chance
in competition with the aggressive forgiveness we call grace.
When it's sin versus grace, grace wins hands down.
All sin can do is threaten us with death, and that's the end of it.
Grace, because God is putting everything together again
through the Messiah, invites us into life—
a life that goes on and on and on, world without end.
—Romans 5:20–21 MSG

Because of the blood of Christ, we are bought
and made free from the punishment of sin.
And because of His blood, our sins are forgiven.
His loving-favor to us is so rich.
—Ephesians 1:7 NLV

*W*hen you worry that God's grace will run out on you:

God's law was given so that all people
could see how sinful they were.
But as people sinned more and more, God's
wonderful grace became more abundant.
—Romans 5:20 NLT

Sin is no longer your master, for you no longer
live under the requirements of the law.
Instead, you live under the freedom of God's grace.
—Romans 6:14 NLT

If we are unfaithful, he remains faithful—
for He cannot deny who He is.
—2 Timothy 2:13 NLT

God is able to make all grace overflow to you so that,
in all things and at all times, having all you need,
you will overflow with every good work.
—2 Corinthians 9:8 MOUNCE

For from his fullness we have all received,
grace upon grace.
—John 1:16 ESV

Acknowledgments

O h, so many extraordinary people to thank.

To my agent, Andrew Wolgemuth. I'm so grateful for your commitment to excellence, your integrity and thoughtfulness, and the way your love for the Gospel is woven into everything you do. It's an honor to be represented by you.

To Ami McConnell. The most ridiculous smile spreads across my face when I think back to how obvious God was when He ensured our paths crossed. (Thank you, Patti Henry!) I'm forever grateful for the God-ordained evening that ultimately led to our partnership on this book. Thank you for loving this book and being so excited about the message of grace within it. Thank you for the good work you started. Your fingerprints are all over these pages!

To my editor, Philis Boultinghouse. It has been pure joy to partner with you. This book would not be what it is now—not even close—without your expertise, heart, and wisdom. You have worked tirelessly to get us to the finish line with a message we can be so very proud of and one that will impact both new moms and grandmothers alike. Also, to Jonathan Merkh and the entire team at Howard Books, thank you so much for making this such an enjoyable journey!

To the incredible team at LifeWay. I am over-the-moon about

partnering with you to create a Bible Study to complement this book. I know moms are going to be so blessed by the opportunity to gather in community to share their own stories, receive much-needed encouragement, and dive deeper into the Bible verses that are woven throughout this book. Thank you!

To my faithful friend, Elisabeth Hasselbeck. Your friendship blesses me beyond description. And how incredibly kind has God been to forge a sweet friendship between our families. Thank you for always pointing me to Jesus and never letting me forget that we have an audience of One. You are wise and loyal and humble and hilarious and prayerful and generous and gracious. You inspire me and challenge me and remind me that all really is grace. I love you for who you are, and I'm so grateful for what you've done in supporting the message within these pages.

To my faithful friend, Courtney DeFeo. Quite simply, I adore you. Thank you for allowing me to borrow your courage when I've wanted to quit and for loving me through my crazy. You never judge, always love, and continually keep me encouraged. I am ridiculously honored to call you my friend and to be on this journey alongside you. I seriously don't know what I'd do without you. I love you, Court.

To Nicole Zasowski, Barb Morris, Stephanie Harbour, Julia Eberwein, Jennifer Meredith, Blair Zamacona, Elizabeth Epley, Lindsey Snedeker, Jodie Berndt, Allison Hendrix, Melanie Dale, and Lauretta Haugh, and the beautiful souls in my morning Bible study. To my ever-faithful Morella Atkinson, Heidi Hutchinson, and Heather Taylor. You have each contributed to this book in profound and unique ways. From the bottom of my heart, thank you for graciously offering your stories, wisdom, encouragement, and prayers. I cherish your friendship, and I love you.

To my Trinity Church family, a community of authentic believers who bless our family beyond measure. We love doing life with you. Better said, we wouldn't survive without you! And special thanks to Hillary Bercovici for kindly lending me your ear when I've needed it most and for allowing me to borrow your term "merciless critic" in this book. And special thanks to Drew Williams and Andy Hayball for allowing me to share your wisdom in these pages.

To my parents, Bonnie and George Callahan. Of all the things you gave me and all the sacrifices you made for me, I am most grateful that you gave me the gift of growing up in a home where the Gospel was everything. You gave me grace and modeled freedom in Christ. Your endless support of me and your gladness about the work God has given me to do spurs me on. I don't take for granted the sacrifices you've made to care for and love on my boys when I've needed to hide away in my office to write, and to travel to speak. I love you so much.

To my sisters and my best friends, Patti Callahan Henry and Barbi Burris. As the Irish expression goes, "I smile because you're my sisters. I laugh because there's nothing you can do about it." Your love and support make me brave. I admire you and love you both so much.

To my hubby. You slay me, Mike Cunnion. Your faith, courage, sense of humor, compassion, integrity, wisdom, selflessness, humility, natural fatherly instincts, unconditional love, tender eyes, and gorgeous face slay me. You lead and love our family so well, and you set the most extraordinary example for our boys. Thank you for your ceaseless support and encouragement. I could never (ever!) do this without you. You're my person, and I love you with all my heart.

To Cal, Brennan, Owen, and Finn. Raising you, alongside your dad, is truly the greatest joy and privilege of my life. *I love us.* There is nothing I enjoy more than doing life as the six of us—I love cheering you on in your games from the sidelines, taking our dogs on long hikes, cuddling on the couch while watching TV, throwing a football on the beach, and reading the Bible and praying in bed each night with you. The truth is, being the mom I long to be for you is more challenging than I ever imagined it would be, and as you well know I need a lot of do-overs and forgiveness. But I'm so grateful that God is faithful to use my imperfections, along with your imperfections, to teach us more and more about His perfect grace for us both. I love who each of you are, and I love who each of you are becoming. May you always know how much I treasure the gift of being your mom and how much I love watching you continue to grow more and more into the God-loving men He created you to be. And finally, as we pray each morning, "I pray that Christ may live in your hearts by faith. I pray that you will be filled with love. I pray that you will be able to understand how wide and how long and how high and how deep His love is. I pray that you will know the love of Christ. His love goes beyond anything we can understand. I pray that you will be filled with God Himself" (Ephesians 3:17-19 NLV).

To Jesus Christ, my Lord and Savior and Best Friend. May I never, ever lose the wonder of Your love—an indescribable love that I've attempted to express in these pages, to the glory of Your grace. May this book be a sweet love song to You, and may it serve as a catalyst to help moms walk in the wild freedom for which You have set us free. You are my everything, and I count all things but loss for the surpassing worth of knowing you (Philippians 3:8).

Notes

CHAPTER 2

1. *ESV Gospel Transformation Bible* commentary on Proverbs 22:6: *The ESV Gospel Transformation Bible* (Wheaton, IL: Crossway, 2013), p. 822.
2. https://www.washingtonpost.com/local/making-time-for-kids -study-says-quality-trumps-quantity/2015/03/28/10813192-d378 -11e4-8fce-3941fc548f1c_story.html.

CHAPTER 3

1. http://annvoskamp.com/2016/05/25-things-every-growing -up-graduating-kid-their-parents-needs-to-know/.

CHAPTER 5

1. My pastor, Drew Williams, said this in a sermon and gave me permission to quote.

CHAPTER 6

1. https://www.thegospelcoalition.org/article/why-youth-stay-in -church-when-they-grow-up , written by Jon Nielson, and published by The Gospel Coalition.

CHAPTER 8

1. Timothy Keller, *The Meaning of Marriage: Facing the Complexities of Commitment with the Wisdom of God* (New York: Penguin Group, 2011), p. 40 .

2. Brennan Manning, *The Ragamuffin Gospel* (Colorado Springs: Mult-nomah Books, 2005), p. 25.

CHAPTER 9

1. http://brenebrown.com/2013/01/14/2013114shame-v-guilt-html/.
2. http://www.oprah.com/own-super-soul-sunday/Oprah-and-Brené-Brown.
3. http://www.relevantmagazine.com/life/real-reason-shame-destroys-your-life#Odg2Vm2s3hfGDqOx.99.

CHAPTER 10

1. Brennan Manning, *The Ragamuffin Gospel* (Colorado Springs: Mult-nomah Books, 2005) p. 87.
2. Manning, *The Ragamuffin Gospel*, p. 28.
3. Elyse Fitzpatrick, *Good News for Weary Women* (Carol Stream, IL: Tyndale House Publishers, 2014), pp. 172–74.

CHAPTER 11

1. Daniel Montgomery and Timothy Paul Jones, *Proof* (Grand Rapids: Zondervan, 2014), p. 79.
2. C. F. W. Walther, *Law and Gospel* (Saint Louis: Concordia Publishing House, 2010), p. 23.
3. Walther, *Law and Gospel*, p. 23.
4. http://www.paultripp.com/articles/posts/walk-in-a-manner-worthy.
5. ESV commentary, 1620.

CHAPTER 12

1. http://www.christianitytoday.com/moi/2000/001/january/lincoln-at-slave-block.html.
2. Martin Luther, *Commentary on Galatians* (Grand Rapids: Kregel Publications, 1987).
3. Elyse Fitzpatrick, *Good News for Weary Women* (Carol Stream, IL: Tyndale House Publishers, 2014), pp. 118–20.
4. Study note on John 6:22–59.

CHAPTER 14

1. Jack Klumpenhower, *Show Them Jesus* (Greensboro, NC: New Growth Press, 2014), p. 39.
2. https://www.thegospelcoalition.org/article/why-youth-stay-in-church-when-they-grow-up, written by Jon Nielson, and published by The Gospel Coalition.

CHAPTER 15

1. http://qz.com/642351/is-the-way-we-parent-causing-a-mental-health-crisis-in-our-kids/.
2. http://www.theatlantic.com/magazine/archive/2015/12/the-silicon-valley- suicides/413140/.
3. https://www.keylife.org/articles/sally-lloyd-jones-teach-children-the-bible-isnt-about-them.
4. Henri Nouwen, *Life of the Beloved* (New York: The Crossroad Publishing Company, 2002), p. 45.

CHAPTER 16

1. https://fulleryouthinstitute.org/blog/warmth-in-your-family.
2. http://www.paultripp.com/assets/1804/video_transcript_grace_liberates_our_parenting.pdf.

CHAPTER 17

1. http://www.desiringgod.org/art.

CHAPTER 18

1. https://www.barna.com/research/barna-studies-the-research-offers-a-year-in-review-perspective/#.

CONNECT WITH
Jeannie

JeannieCunnion.com | 📷 @JeannieCunnion
🐦 @JeannieCunnion | 📘 /JeannieCunnion

Connect with fellow *Mom Set Free* fans or share your
favorite thoughts from the book at #MomSetFree.

PROUDLY PUBLISHED BY Ⓗ HOWARD BOOKS®
AN IMPRINT OF SIMON & SCHUSTER, INC.
A CBS COMPANY

58421

Your kids aren't perfect. And you don't have to be either.

Are you exhausted from the pressure to be a perfect parent raising perfect children in this imperfect world? Do you ever wonder, 'How did these precious children get stuck with a parent like me?' If so, let these grace-drenched pages saturate your heart with God's unfailing love while also equipping you to be a vessel of God's unconditional love to your children.

With authenticity, conviction, and a lively sense of humor, Jeannie guides you on a transformative journey into raising wholehearted—not perfect—children, who live from the freedom found in being wholeheartedly loved (and liked!) by God.

Parenting the Wholehearted Child equips you with biblical wisdom and practical ideas to teach your children that they are fully accepted by God, not because of anything they do or don't do but because of everything Jesus has already done for them.

Woven throughout the book is the good news that it is God's extravagant grace—not your perfect performance—that transforms the hearts of children.